Finding Mom

Finding Mom

Stephen C. Messer

RESOURCE *Publications* · Eugene, Oregon

FINDING MOM

Resource Publications
An Imprint of Wipf and Stock Publishers
199 W. 8th Ave., Suite 3
Eugene, OR 97401

www.wipfandstock.com

ISBN 13: 978-1-4982-0810-9

Manufactured in the U.S.A.   02/02/2015

For my parents

Marian Bertha Pett Messer (1928–1961)

and

Jarvis Norman Messer (1929–2012)

RIP

Table of Contents

PROLOGUE

September 20, 1961

I LEANED AGAINST THE bedroom door; something thumped. I leaned again, pushed it open and walked in. I found my mother hanging on the back side with belts around her contorted face. She didn't respond to my cry. I turned, ran down the stairs screaming "emergency" and grabbed my neck with both hands to show my father what I had seen. It was September 20, 1961; I was six years old; and my mother, Marian Pett Messer, had committed suicide.

Wednesday, September 20, 1961 started as a normal day in our life as a Navy family in Sasebo, Japan. I don't remember anything about the morning and early afternoon. Since I had just started first grade three weeks earlier, I must have taken the bus from our off-base quarters to my school on the base and returned around 2:30 pm. According to a letter my mother wrote to my great aunt that morning, Kazuko, our maid, did the laundry while she worked on preparing dinner. Sometime that afternoon, my mother mailed this letter, most likely during the drive she and I took to the harbor to pick up my father who had just returned from a deployment aboard the USS *Ajax*. Dad remembers my mother being more talkative than usual on the ride back to our quarters. Upon our return home, she said she was going upstairs to rest and Dad and I should work on the model airplanes we had started building before this most recent voyage; if we were hungry, there were hamburgers made up in the refrigerator. As she went up the stairs, she stopped and told my father that it was good that we were going to work on our planes together since "Steve needs you now." I don't remember working on our planes, and I don't remember eating the hamburgers. I do remember one of my mother's friends coming to the door and asking to see her. Dad asked me to go upstairs and let her know that our neighbor was there.

As I ran screaming down the stairs, my father rushed past me, pulled my mother down and frantically tried to revive her. The details blur at this point. I vaguely remember an ambulance arriving and the corpsmen taking my mother to the base hospital while I stayed at home with our neighbor. I vividly remember cleaning up the kitchen table, going outside to pick a flower, and then putting this flower on the table so that my mother would be happy when she returned.

She didn't return.

After some time, Dad did return and took me to the hospital to see my mother one last time. He began to explain to me that she had died. At the hospital, we entered a room, and her body was on a bed. Because of preparations by the staff, her face was now peaceful—as if she were asleep. Dad then took me to a fellow officer's house where we would spend the next two nights. At some point during the evening, he took me out to the backyard. We sat at a picnic table as he talked to me about what had happened and tried to help me understand that my mother was no longer with us.

My memories of this horrific day end with a gripping experience of grace in the midst of my shock. As Dad faced me and tried to comfort me while dealing with his own terrible grief and bewilderment, I looked over his left shoulder and saw a brilliantly illuminated figure walking toward the trees at the end of the yard. I remember not knowing who or what it was. Was it my mother's spirit? Was it Jesus? Was it an angel? I didn't know then, and I don't know with certainty now. However, I did know with certainty then that in the midst of my searing pain and fear, I felt deeply cared for. I didn't tell anyone about this figure until years later; it became my secret.

My secret about the illuminated figure was the first of a multitude that followed my mother's suicide. I didn't tell Dad about the figure until May of 2011. There are other family members and close friends who will learn about it only when they read these words. However, the biggest secret of my life was that my mother *did* commit suicide. Of course, I knew she had hanged herself, as did every adult in my family. I recalled September 20, 1961 often; to this day I can't speak the word "emergency" without remembering how I screamed it running down those stairs. But it was 1961, and most Americans didn't deal openly with death, and those in respectable Christian families like ours definitely didn't talk about suicide or seek professional help in dealing with it. People who loved me dearly and cared for me unselfishly didn't discuss it because they wanted to protect me from my own memories and from the social stigma attached to the survivors of suicide. I therefore learned at a young age not to mention this topic. When I was about eight years old and living with my grandparents, I told my grandmother that I had shared the story of how my mother died with two of my neighborhood playmates. She immediately and firmly told me not to talk to my friends about my mother's death. My grandmother loved me deeply, so deeply that she and my grandfather raised me from 1961 until I went to college in 1973. But she taught me a powerful lesson that day, and I learned this lesson well. I learned it so well that at times I lied about how my mother died. On those rare occasions when I as a child, adolescent, or young adult mentioned her death to someone outside my family, I often said she died in an accident or a fall. I learned this lesson so well that I tried my hardest to live my life as if my mother's suicide had not really happened; I just wanted the trauma to go away. As a result of the wall my family built around my mother's death and our efforts to maintain it, the second biggest secret in my life became who my mother really was. Because we rarely spoke about her, my clearest and most frequent memory of her was the body hanging on that door. If I asked a direct question about her, I would get a direct answer; but I had to initiate these exchanges, and I quickly learned that they were at worst taboo or at best very awkward. The path of least resistance and superficial comfort in 1961, and as I grew up, was silence.

The title of this book reflects the fact that after I found my mother on September 20, 1961, I soon lost her in what my father recently labeled the "decades of silence" that followed. For the next fifty years, I basically followed this path. To be sure, there were times when I mentioned my mother, and especially as I reached young adulthood and the beginning of middle age, I began opening up in small ways. I quit lying about how she died; I had several counseling sessions that touched on her death; and on rare occasions, I briefly shared about her suicide in an effort to comfort others who had survived the suicide of a family member or friend. But other than infrequent discussions with Betty, my wife, I did not talk about my mother with family members; in short, I still had a gaping hole in my life because I did not know who my mother was beyond her death. Because her death did not go away, it remained a foundational part of my life and identity, but her life was not. In many ways, I was still that confused and scared six year old boy fearfully waiting in the kitchen for his mother to return.

The title of this book also reflects the fact that through the journey described in the following pages, I once again found my mother. But this time, I found a fully human woman living her life instead of that contorted figure hanging on the back side of that bedroom door. This time, I found a woman who struggled with severe depression and shattered expectations but who was also passionate about downhill skiing, relished fudge and Whitman's chocolate, listened to Bach, Beethoven *and* Elvis, danced up tempo to *Mack the Knife*, played bridge and tennis, read Thomas Hardy novels, thoroughly enjoyed travel, and loved being a nurse. This time, I found the complex woman who loved me as her son. This time, I found my mom.

Introduction

THE JOURNEY I AM about to describe, and it was both a literal and spiritual journey, began on March 16, 2011, my fifty-sixth birthday. I spent the day feeling physically ill and depressed, and at some point in my distress, I realized with a start that it had been fifty years since I had spent my last birthday with my mother on March 16, 1961. I remembered nothing about my sixth birthday, but I couldn't ignore that it was the last one we had together. As I continued brooding over this realization while driving to work on March 17th, I suddenly knew I needed to devote the time between then and the fiftieth anniversary of my mother's death to getting to know who she really was. After I tearfully blurted out this realization, my wife, Betty, gave her immediate and enthusiastic support, even though on one level it was out of the blue. As a Christian, I have no doubt that the epiphany to undertake this effort was the result of the Lord's "still small voice." It was still and small, but it was also unmistakable. There was no brilliantly illuminated figure this time; it was as if he simply whispered to me "Steve, it's time."

But there were other influences as well. As a historian of United States History, I often focus on significant historical anniversaries in my classes, and during the spring of 2011, a number of these commemorations converged. The Civil War began 150 years ago; Ronald Reagan was born one hundred years ago; JFK's inauguration, the Freedom Rides, and Yuri Gagarin and Alan Shepherd's historic space flights all happened fifty years ago. These historic anniversaries and the catastrophic earthquake and tsunami on March 11, 2011, which focused my attention on the suffering and courage of the Japanese people and by extension on my time in Sasebo, all reinforced this call to get to know my mother as the fiftieth anniversary of her death approached. This book documents what I did for these six months as I attempted to come to terms with what happened on the afternoon of September 20, 1961 and its subsequent impact on my life. I've taken many journeys as a survivor of suicide. On March 17, 2011 I set out on a journey to find my mom for the second time. I began writing her daily letters–letters that told her how I felt and what I experienced as a survivor of her suicide, letters that simply told her about what she had missed as I grew up, and letters that detailed my efforts to find out who she really was. Betty and I took seven road trips between March 17th and September 20th 2011. Our destinations stretched from Ilion, New York, my mother's hometown, to Long Beach, California, our last place of residence before we went to Japan in 1960, to Polo, Illinois, where I grew up after her death, and to many points in between. We visited twenty-four sites specifically connected to her life. I interviewed thirty-one people who knew my mother, examined over 120 photographs and one 8 mm film that visually documented her life, and read thirty-seven letters that she wrote to relatives. I secured copies of her high school and nursing school academic transcripts and yearbooks, and I analyzed fourteen physical artifacts from different stages of her life. As a historian, I found more primary sources that I ever imagined; as a son, I recreated memories that allowed me to find my mother for the first time in fifty years. My letter to her on March 18th conveys my feelings as I began this journey by returning to her grave in Jordanville, New York:

Dear Mom,

> *I'm off tomorrow to your grave. I know you're not there, but there still is some sort of connection there. My goal between now and the 50th anniversary of your death on September 20th is to find out who you were and perhaps find out who you, Dad, and I were as a family. I really need more (and hopefully better) memories of you. Even as a middle-aged, perhaps late middle-aged, adult, I still struggle in the depths of my soul with how we ended as*

a family. I think of you almost every day—and every ten years or so I fall apart struggling with how it ended. I'm tired—deeply weary of this struggle; I know the pain will never totally be gone, but I want to know you—to remember you—for more than the way it ended.

I need more than the image of you hanging on the back of the door, of running down the stairs yelling "emergency" (I still often think of this moment when I use this word.), of Dad's desperate efforts to revive you, of the ambulance, of Dad taking me to see your body at the hospital. I've lived with these memories for almost fifty years, and I've struggled with them, with you, with the way it ended. I don't want it to end there; it can no longer end there. Tomorrow perhaps we can build new memories out of the past—but not this past.

Love your son,

Steve

A photograph I found early in my research visually illustrates my words in this letter and captures what I am trying to do with this book. It is a candid shot most likely taken by Vernie Esterly, my great aunt, during the summer of 1956. My mom and dad are in my grandparents' backyard in Polo, Illinois hanging laundry (which no doubt included my diapers!) out to dry.

The wind is blowing and my parents face away from the camera as they focus on securing the clothing to the line. Their body language indicates both are relaxed, but my mother has her arms extended and seems about to soar on the breeze. When I first saw this photo, I realized it was a powerful visual representation of my overriding goal—to see my mother for the first time in life rather than death and in joy rather than sorrow. This picture not only provided historical evidence about a specific time and a specific place; it reminded me that my quest was to reach out and turn my mother gently around so she faces me, look into her eyes, and draw her close.

The Polo Paradox

MARIAN PETT MESSER'S LIFE slipped away during the "decades of silence" between 1961 and 2011. Before I recount in detail my journey to get to know her again, these decades need explanation and elaboration, and this part of my story begins far from Sasebo in the farm country of northwestern Illinois.

Polo, Illinois is foundational in my life because it became my hometown after my mother's death. I moved there immediately after her funeral, and I lived with my paternal grandparents for twelve years until I left to attend college in 1973. My years growing up in Polo paradoxically made this current effort to get to know my mother both necessary *and* possible. It was necessary because the silence that began immediately following her death continued among my family, friends, and acquaintances in Polo; it was possible because when I finally addressed this silence, one foundation for doing so was the life I experienced in this small farm town. I learned the lesson of silence there, but I also learned other, more positive lessons that sustained me and eventually prepared me to break the silence.

My hometown with its population of approximately 2500 is located in the farm country of northwestern Illinois forty-five miles southwest of Rockford, twelve miles north of Dixon and six miles west of the White Pines State Park. Jarvis and Naomi Esterly Messer, my paternal grandparents, courted in the Polo area during the early 1920s, were married there in 1923, and, following their epic struggles during the Great Depression, returned in 1942 to raise their three children: my father, Norman, my Aunt Bernadyne, and my Uncle Ronald. I became the fourth Messer child to grow up in Polo. When I relate the story of my life, people often ask why I went to Polo after my mother's death. The answer to this question is both straightforward and complex. Part of it relates to my father's suffering. Due to his intense shock, grief, and anger, he was in no shape to raise me on his own in the days and months that followed my mother's death. He went from the steady rhythms of naval and family life through the upheaval of my mother's shocking suicide to difficult decisions about how to care for me and himself. As bewildered as I was, he was living a personal hell that even today I can only imagine. So, one reason I went to Polo was my grandparents' offer to help Dad through this awful time in our lives. A second reason was the Navy's compassionate decision to station my father at the Great Lakes Naval Training Center, which is located north of Chicago and approximately one hundred ten miles east of Polo. Once Dad reported for duty after an extended emergency leave, he was close enough to spend weekends in Polo with me.

But Polo was also my mother's choice. During a visit there for Thanksgiving of 1959, the last of many such family gatherings during the 1950s,[1] she asked my grandparents to take care of me if anything happened to her and Dad was unable to raise me on his own. She did not tell others of this request—neither my father nor her family members in New York, but my grandparents cryptically mentioned it to me several times as I grew up. Although subsequent events make this request seem like a premonition on my mother's part, I can only speculate about it based on the limited evidence I have from this period in her life. By late 1959, she knew we would be leaving our home in Long Beach, California for Sasebo, Japan sometime during the spring of 1960. She had also established a close relationship with my father's parents and his

---

1. My Aunt Bernadyne noted that my grandfather was adamant that the family should gather together for this holiday before we left for Japan. In fact, she noted he was unusually pushy on this issue.

aunt since her marriage into the family in 1952. And then there were her visits. I have numerous photographs of my mother in Polo from Christmas of 1953 through Thanksgiving of 1959.

Christmas in Polo, 1953. This is one of my favorite pictures of my parents. The quality of the image is poor, but their love and joy are crystal clear.

My mother holding me when the circus with those scary elephants came to Polo in 1958.

Thanksgiving in Polo, 1959. We are preparing for the long drive
back to Long Beach, California.

Although these pictures were obviously posed, my mother appears
relaxed and is often smiling. Other photos show her at the family
homestead owned by my Aunt Vernie, and she clearly felt at ease
there. In addition, I have thirty-seven letters that my mother wrote
to my grandparents, my great aunt, and other relatives between
1952 and September 20, 1961, when she penned her last letter to
Aunt Vernie. These letters indicate a close relationship, but one
expressed mainly through sharing the details of everyday life and
holiday celebrations. My mother does not share her feelings, other
than the fatigue she often felt trying to keep up with me and my
exuberant band of friends, her difficulty dealing with hot weather,
and her frustration with the Navy's approach to duty assignments
for my father. Even in the letter she wrote my aunt on the morning
of her suicide, she does not reveal any clear sense of depression or
angst. In addition to mentioning what she and Kazuko were doing,
she notes that the summer heat had broken enough to once again
sleep with blankets and without fans, comments on the progress

Aunt Vernie had reported with her garden, and remarks that Dad's new orders would not come through until the following spring. Although there is no overt hint of a decision to take her life, the fact that she did write her last letter to my aunt and that she left no suicide note even though she clearly planned her death,[2] indicates her sense of connection and closeness to her Polo family and especially with my Aunt Vernie.[3] Given my mother's professional training as a nurse and the fact that she had shown definite signs of serious depression during our years in Long Beach, she may have sensed she might not return from Japan. Given what family members have told me about her devotion to me, this feeling may have led her to initiate this quiet conversation with my grandparents. Many unanswered questions swirl around her request. Exactly what did my mother sense about her own condition? Why did she choose my paternal grandparents rather than her parents? Why did she feel that Dad might not be able to take care of me on his own? But one point is clear—my grandparents took this conversation seriously and lived out their affirmative response for the rest of their lives.

There is one more issue to address concerning why I grew up in Polo, and that is why I did not return to live with Dad at some point after the initial shock of my mother's death dissipated. The key reasons were my comfort and Dad's instability. After a few years, I became very comfortable living with my grandparents;

2. I support my father's conclusion that my mother did plan her suicide based on her comment before going upstairs, her decision to leave her Bible on the bed open to Ecclesiastes, chapter 3:2 ("a time to be born and a time to die.") and the comment of the doctor who performed her autopsy who noted that she had committed the "perfect hanging" in that it was quick and lethal because of the way she set it up.

3. This letter provides a telling example of the pervasive silence about my mother. Although my Aunt Vernie was very close to me during my Polo years and lived until 1995, she never told me about this letter or any of the other letters she had received from my mother. She also never shared her numerous photos of my mother in Polo. Fortunately, my siblings Aimee and Molly found these letters and photographs when going through family papers after my grandmother's death in 1998 and saved them. I first became aware of them during the spring of 2011.

their home became my home. This sense of stability contrasted sharply with the ongoing instability in Dad's life. By the mid-1960s, Dad had escaped his abuse of alcohol without becoming an alcoholic, but after a quick remarriage and an equally quick divorce, he had remarried for the second time. He and his new wife began having their own children, and it was painfully obvious she would not welcome me into their growing family. I was a living reminder that Dad had a life—and a complicated one at that—prior to meeting her, and this was an issue she adamantly and vocally refused to address in a constructive fashion. We did try visits and short trips as a blended family during several summers. However, it was soon clear that my very presence inflamed her, and as a result, I was reluctant to leave my home in Polo to live with someone I feared because I felt she hated me. After several conversations as I approached my teen years, Dad and I agreed, regretfully on his part but with relief on mine, that it was best for me to remain in Polo with my grandparents. And so, these broader family dynamics finalized the decision that had been only temporary immediately after my mother's death.

As I noted earlier, Polo was a place of both silence and significant growth for me. The silence about my mother was pervasive. I very quickly learned that her death was a topic that made people uncomfortable and which they wished to avoid. I now know that the adults in my life were sincerely and understandably concerned about reawakening my memories of that awful day and about the social stigma I would face if people knew. However, although this environment taught me to avoid speaking about my mother, I thought about her almost every day *and* I constantly wondered who knew. Who knew about my mother and her death? Did my friends at school and church know that I was the son of a suicide? Did anyone looking at me and speaking in hushed tones know my secret?

I did my part to keep this secret by maintaining my own silence. I rarely mentioned my mother, and I almost never asked questions about her life or death. I intentionally ignored the two pictures of her that my grandmother placed on my bedroom bookshelf. For years, I avoided going downstairs to the basement as much as possible because my mother's personal items from Japan were stored in a back corner, and I was scared to be there alone. I'm not sure my grandparents ever figured out why I usually ran up the basement stairs, and if they had asked, I most likely would have made up a reason for my hasty and noisy exits. The following letter to my mother addressed this issue as I attempted to come to terms with this fear as an adult.

3/31/2011

Dear Mom,

    One early memory from Polo is the arrival of our stuff from Japan. I remember the big boxes on the front lawn and some furniture, including the green speckled couch you were sitting on in one of the pictures from Japan. Most of the things went to the back of the basement, and most of them stayed unopened there until Grandma Messer died in 1998.

    Sometimes I would go back there and look at these things as I grew up, but for the most part I felt sort of eerie around them. There were times I wouldn't go to the basement because of this feeling and other times I didn't want to be there alone. I guess being around all these things from our life together in Japan at times reminded me of how our life together ended.

    But there were some good memories associated with some items. I did continue playing in my mock sailboat for several years. And there was this small wooden box that I had played with in Japan. Some sort of spice cake came in the box, and for years, I could still smell that cake.

    I also found some of your personal items—like your jewelry box and billfold. At some point in my adult life I threw both away—I really don't know why; but I did keep your nursing pin and Grandma Messer made sure I kept your string of pearls. I'm carrying your nursing pin with me during this time; it now feels good to have a reminder of you with me.

                            Love your son,

                                   Steve

After my initial conversation about my mother's death with two of my neighborhood playmates and my grandmother's definitive response, I did not tell my close friends about her, nor did I mention her to pastors, Sunday school teachers, or youth group leaders. On those rare occasions when I mentioned her to family members, I never talked about the hole I had in my life because of her physical and emotional absence. I never mentioned my questions about how she died, why she left me, and whether I had something to do with her decision to take her life. I never asked my dad any questions about our life together as a family. And I never shared my encounter with the illuminated figure even though my memory of this moment reminded me over and over again that God did care about me.

As I now look back on my years in Polo, I realize that because I followed the path of silence and did all that I could to keep my mother's suicide a secret, doing so exacted a serious emotional toll on me. As noted, I always wondered who knew. My constant scrutiny of those around me for clues as to whether or not they knew impacted me in a number of ways. I developed a limited sense of trust since I always felt that I could not share my deepest pain, even with those who were very close to me. I consistently placed a boundary around how open I was about my feelings, even with those who cared deeply about my well-being, and I still struggle with these issues of trust and openness as an adult. In addition, my self-esteem took a beating. On top of the normal challenges a young person faces in this area, I added uncertainty about my worth due to being the son of someone who committed suicide. I took criticism much more to heart than praise, and I became deeply self-critical. As a result, I sought relief and solace in perfectionism. I clearly remember feeling that I needed to be perfect in order to keep my place in my new family and my new home. I had lost my mother and a normal relationship with my father; I therefore felt compelled to be the perfect grandson so I wouldn't lose Grandma and Grandpa and my life in my new hometown.

I also had what are now recognized as normal reactions from a person who loses a loved one to suicide, but because of the silence (and the total lack of professional counseling due to this silence), I had no idea I was feeling emotions that were to be expected for someone who had witnessed what I had witnessed. The most obvious example of this response was my anger. Throughout my life, I have had an issue with anger, although I kept this emotion under wraps more often than not. The problem was that I usually stifled this intense emotion by burying it and neither acknowledging it nor dealing with it. It would then burst out in unexpected and often unacceptable ways such as yelling, fighting, or stomping away from challenging situations. In order to address these outbursts (remember the perfectionism), I would seek to bury the anger even deeper in the hope that it would go away. It rarely did. What I missed completely until recently is that I was angry at my mother for leaving me in the way she did and for how her decision affected my subsequent relationship with my father. I was angry at my father for raising his new family but not me. I was angry because on a very basic level, I felt abandoned and was worried that it would happen again

As a result of all this stress, I would often have days which ran the gamut from intense effort to get everything right to extreme despair when I didn't. As a seven year old, I remember jumping from the edge of a wet bathtub in an effort to punish myself physically because I felt that my father, who was present for a weekend visit, was upset with me. As a young Sunday school student, I remember feeling that I had to start my nightly prayers over from the very beginning if I mispronounced a single syllable. Surely God didn't care about my pronunciation, but I acted as though he was grading my diction rather than listening to my soul. As a high school student, I remember deciding to quit the golf team because I couldn't handle the combination of my perfectionism and temper. Bending my putter into a horseshoe-like shape after missing a short putt caught even my attention, and I turned my back on a game I had grown to love. In addition to all the expected strains of childhood and adolescence, I developed an internal life dedicated to suppressing the real cause of these behavioral traits—finding my mother on the back of that bedroom door.

And I still didn't know who knew. Although I no longer fret about this issue, I recently discovered that a close friend from Polo did know that my mother had died, but not that she had taken her life; another close friend knew that she had committed suicide but not that I had found her. I'm sure that Mrs. Muench, my first grade teacher, knew some of the details since she would have received an explanation when I suddenly showed up as a new student in her classroom in mid-October of 1961. My guess is that a number of key people in my life including teachers, school administrators, pastors, friends, and neighbors, did know part of my story, but they too maintained the silence to protect me. I have no doubt that some Poloans who knew me as I grew up will read this book and recall what they knew and what they didn't, and others will become aware of my circumstances for the first time. Although this silence surely had negative consequences for me (and for others such as Dad who needed counseling as much as I did), it reflected the reality of dealing with death, and especially suicide, in the early 1960s. I am frustrated that nobody initiated a sustained conversation with me about my mother, about what I had witnessed, or about who she really was. Given the journey described in this book, I often wonder how speaking openly about my mother or taking a father and son road trip to places associated with her life would have impacted me as a youth. I still struggle with the fact that deceased loved ones had letters and pictures they never shared with me and that those still living did not share their material and memories until I inquired about them in 2011. But I also have no doubt that those who perpetuated this silence did so with the best of motives and the deepest sense of concern for me. Given the time and the place, they did what they thought was best for me. My hope is that telling my story will encourage others experiencing similar trauma today to consider breaking their silence in order to openly and constructively address the secrets that burden them.

At the beginning of this chapter I noted that Polo is significant in my life not only for this silence, but also for giving me a foundation to challenge it. The same level of care that family members and friends expressed by keeping my mother's death and life so quiet also encouraged me to develop in ways that eventually allowed me to breach this silence. As I now look back on my time in Polo as a middle-aged adult on this journey, I see this paradoxical outcome as rooted in the stability, love, faith, and friendship I experienced in this small mid-western town.

Although I felt deeply insecure as a result of my mother's death and its aftermath, my insecurity was tempered by a sense of stability that grew slowly over the years. In one sense, Polo itself was a model of stability; the population had neither increased nor decreased significantly since its founding as a railroad boom town in 1857, and at times it appeared like the backdrop for a series of iconic Norman Rockwell paintings. The tree lined streets in the autumn featured brightly colored piles of fallen leaves for joyful play and pungent fires; winter revealed the beauty of deep and sculpted snow drifts during quiet muffled walks to and from school; spring provided wild violets growing along the sidewalks and the gentle new growth on trees and in the budding gardens peaking from neighbors' backyards; summer brought the comforting drone of lawn mowers by day and excess tomato exchanges while visiting in the cool evenings. All of these qualities promoted a rhythm of stability, as did the routines of my life. I mowed lawns, hung out with my new friends, played Little League baseball, and sharpened my golf and tennis skills in the summer; I raked leaves, played sandlot football, sold pumpkins, gathered bittersweet, celebrated homecoming, and went trick or treating in the fall; I shoveled snow, went sledding (complete with a roaring fire and a kettle of hot chocolate at the top of the hill!), and built forts for intricately planned and hotly contested snowball campaigns in the winter; and I planted trees and flowers, celebrated May Day with brightly colored baskets, and cleaned out the garage and the basement in the spring. These seasonal patterns quieted and comforted me as I settled in to a new life.

The daily love my grandparents and great aunt gave me undergirded and fortified my slowly growing sense of stability. They not only took me in at a terrible time in my life, they did so with enthusiasm. They showed their love in both action and attitude. On the action front, Aunt Vernie (who was well into her sixties when I arrived) played endless games of softball, croquet, and Monopoly with me, initiated me into the secrets of her garden and orchard, and introduced me to her towering old house, which contained all sorts of old, odd, and interesting artifacts in its endless nooks and crannies. Grandpa patiently taught me how to mow the yard and how to fish; he took me on hikes to gather wild strawberries, hunt for mushrooms, and see the family cabin of his childhood; he became a Little League manager even though baseball clearly was not one of his passions; and he took up golf at the age of sixty-one so he could spend more time with me. As I grew older, but long before my formal drivers' education course in high school, he taught me to drive as he collected soil samples in the wide open fields he analyzed for his farmer clients. Grandma took me to the Polo Library for my first library card (#1612); attended school events such as Christmas programs, book fairs, and sporting events; shuttled me to Cub Scout meetings, swimming lessons, choir practice, and the golf course in her classic 1946 Plymouth; baked a delicious frosted angel food cake each year for my birthday; read Bible stories to me; taught me how to cook, clean, and do laundry; showed me how to color Easter eggs, make May baskets, arrange a homemade Halloween hobo costume, and bake Christmas cookies; gently cleaned and bandaged my numerous scrapes and cuts; and nursed me through what I perceived as endless bouts with childhood diseases.

Beyond these overt demonstrations of their care, my grandparents and aunt articulated an attitude of love for me. I learned that they loved me not only because of all they did for me, but because they told me they loved me. Grandma told me how proud she was of my work in school; she even praised my less than mediocre efforts to make her a gift in art class. Grandpa told me how delighted he was that I could accompany him on fishing expeditions, hikes, trips to the local drive-in for a Black Cow, and occasionally to work. At some point in these journeys, he often started humming *Me and My Shadow* and told me that he was glad that I was his shadow. Aunt Vernie often told me how much she appreciated what I added to the family as we puttered around her house, her shed, and the surrounding grounds. In addition to these words, Grandma, Grandpa, and Aunt Vernie showed their love by keeping tabs on me. They quietly peaked into my room at night to make sure I was sleeping restfully; they routinely asked how my day at school had gone; they looked out of windows to make sure I was enjoying playtime with my friends; and they then asked how my play had gone when I came inside. In today's terminology, they "had my back" during my daily and weekly activities. Even though I continued to feel deeply insecure in many ways in the aftermath of my mother's death, I began to understand that they loved me. Just as I knew that I was cared for when I saw the illuminated figure in Sasebo, I came to sense my grandparents' and aunt's abiding love.

My grandparents, Jarvis and Naomi Messer.

I'm visiting my Aunt Vernie at her house.

Two other family members, my Aunt Bernadyne and Uncle Bill, became special to me during my years in Polo, and my mother actually had something to say about this relationship shortly after I was born in 1955. When Aunt Bernadyne called my mother in the spring of that year to announce her engagement to William "Bill" Snook, my mother replied with her congratulations and noted that this was especially great for me since "every little boy needs an Uncle Bill." Well, it turned out that this little boy really needed an Uncle Bill *and* an Aunt Bernadyne. I first felt a connection with them when they met us in San Francisco when we returned from Japan with my mother's body. Although I remember very little of our hurried and harried journey from Sasebo back to the States, I do remember our trip from the west coast to Ilion, New York for my mother's funeral and burial. We travelled by train, and Aunt Bernadyne spent most of that trip caring for me since Dad spent a good deal of time addressing his shock and grief in the club car. I remember her bathing me, talking to me about the passing scenery, and taking me to the dining car for meals. I remember enjoying her attention and actually having some fun for the first time in days. Aunt Bernadyne and Uncle Bill continued to care for me as I grew older, whether it was welcoming me into their home, spending time with me when they visited Polo, helping to celebrate my birthday and graduation milestones, supporting my interest in music, or encouraging me to take my faith development seriously. They added their love and care to that of my grandparents and great aunt and thereby helped me to develop some semblance of normalcy even though the silence persisted.

Faith was the third foundation for the growth I experienced in Polo. As soon as I began talking, my mother encouraged me to say my prayers before going to bed. One of her favorites was my adaptation of a classic when I prayed "Now I lay me down to sleep . . . for a while." She felt my wording was particularly appropriate because I was always on the move and rarely went to sleep without a struggle. In addition, I learned about Jesus in Japan through Sunday school and Vacation Bible School classes and the stories my mother frequently read to me from a large brown Bible story book with a picture of Christ on the front cover. Without this background, I likely would not have had the context for immediately grasping the caring message the illuminated figure shared with me. But it was in Polo that my Christian faith took root. When I moved there, my grandparents and aunt were active members of Emmanuel Evangelical United Brethren (EUB) Church, and this congregation became my church home. I immediately felt welcomed by these folks, and I quickly became active in Sunday school, Vacation Bible School, youth choir, the acolyte guild, and the youth group. Rev. Len Huff, our pastor, frequently and warmly connected with the youth, and I soon knew him as one of the kindest men I had ever met. I remember enjoying his sermons, the liturgy of the morning service, and my favorite hymns, *Holy, Holy, Holy, Fairest Lord Jesus*, and *For the Beauty of the Earth*. Rev. Huff so impressed me that in second grade I identified becoming a minister as my career goal with the rationale that "you get to help people, and it's a good, clean living." Although I settled enthusiastically into the routines of church life, confirmation was the key experience in the development of my own personal faith. Two weeks before the confirmation service, Rev. Huff reminded us that our time together was not just about learning about the Bible and church history or joining the church and agreeing to support it; it was about making an open and serious faith commitment. He asked us to think about this commitment in light of what we had learned, and if we wished to declare our willingness to follow Jesus, to join him at the altar the following week after our final class session. I recall two defining characteristics of this experience. First, Rev. Huff presented this invitation in such a gentle fashion that there was no intense pressure to comply; it was clearly my decision. Second, I consciously connected this event to the illuminated figure in Sasebo; even though I still had not shared my secret, I knew my decision to follow Jesus was a response to this earlier declaration of divine love and care.

My faith took a number of twists and turns during my remaining years in Polo. I contentedly continued my spiritual development at Emmanuel EUB Church until 1968. At that point, my grandparents left the church in response to the denominational merger with the United Methodists and joined a new, fundamentalist congregation that became the First Baptist Church. My experience at First Baptist was mixed. I appreciated the intensive Bible study, the gusto with which the congregation sang the great hymns of the faith as well as the first generation of what we now call praise songs, the youth activities (including church softball and my first experience at summer camp) and the seriousness these folks had about their faith and their witness. On the other hand, I struggled with the dogmatic sermons and comments that sent the unmistakable message that most of my friends, my *Christian* friends, were wrong about doctrine, church polity, their preferred translation of the Bible, and most likely their salvation. I had an especially hard time dealing with what I perceived to be an emphasis that equated being perfect with true holiness since, as stated earlier, I was already predisposed to carry the burden of perfectionism. As I look back now as a former fundamentalist, I realize my biggest tension was with the message that God was a stern thundering judge who was far more interested in punishment than love. For example, I heard about the so-called unpardonable sin for the first time in my life at this church, and somehow I connected this transgression to suicide, although other possibilities were presented as well. Although I eventually chose not to remain in the fundamentalist fold, I now realize that my time at First Baptist deepened the commitment I made at Emmanuel EUB. As I left Polo to attend college in 1973, I left as a Christian who grasped my need for God's care and love and desired to follow him even though I was unsure about denominational specifics, uncomfortable with Christian legalism, and still struggling with the after effects of my mother's death.

As I grew up in Polo with all of my challenges, I was sustained by the stability, love and faith that become so much a part of my life. However, friendship was the fourth component that made this developmental trio a quartet. Although I did not interact with my closest Polo friends about my mother and her death until I actually began this project, the fact that I still see Jane and Jeff and Becky and Steve and their spouses on a regular basis as we enter our early-sixties is remarkable. It certainly helps that we live only thirty miles apart, but our current relationship is based on much more than proximity. The bond we have today is grounded on what we shared with each other as we grew up in Polo: common classes and teachers (often excellent and occasionally eccentric), marching band trips, formal concerts, pep band performances, different expressions of Christianity, long and frequently intense discussions about the pressing social and political issues of the late 1960s and early 1970s, our college plans, and the fact that most of the time, we just genuinely enjoyed each other's company.

As I reflect on what these friends meant to me then, I come back to the fact that they helped me become a better person. They patiently accepted me when I annoyed them with my intolerant political beliefs and arrogant pronouncements on matters of faith; they encouraged me to develop my academic abilities and appreciation for music; they consistently validated my plans to attend college; and they routinely helped me cut loose and have some fun. Even with the ongoing internal struggles stemming from my mother's death, I knew they, like my grandparents, great aunt, and aunt and uncle would be there for me. We can still act like the kids we once were during our very competitive adult four square games or when we gently mimic our "favorite" high school teacher at a cookout, but we also know at a fundamental level that we respect one another deeply and will, without question, support each other through hard times.

This then is the paradox of Polo. The silence about my mother was pervasive, but I gained the support and began developing the characteristics that eventually contributed to breaking the silence. Without experiencing the stability, love, faith, and friendship during my years in Polo, I most likely would not have made it to where I am today. As my Uncle Ron noted during a recent conversation about my mother and her death, I could have very easily gone off the deep end given what I witnessed as a six year old and did not process as a child and adolescent. But I didn't. Although I internalized my mother's death for fifty years without dealing with it openly, I was able to continue living my life with some sense of normalcy. It certainly was not what it could have been, but I did not go off that deep end. I came to Polo in 1961 as a bewildered and frightened six year old. When I left for college twelve years later, I did so with the ongoing burden of silence but also with a solid foundation for life and a passion for history.

2

History and Me

THE PARADOX OF POLO continued to shape my life from 1973 when I entered Trinity College[1] until I began this journey in 2011. My mother was present only through her suicide and the silence that surrounded it, and at the same time I continued to grow in ways that kept me from falling off that deep end. One of these growth areas was my engagement with the discipline of history. I entered Trinity with a calling to study and teach history, a calling which began in Polo and shaped my educational journey as a young adult, and more importantly, a calling which led me down paths that continued preparing me to break the silence.

My love of history is rooted in reading, and I've enjoyed reading as long as I can remember. In one of my mother's letters, she mentions reading me a new book five times in one day because I was so engaged with its story. Before we left for Japan she purchased the *Children's Britannica Encyclopedia* for me and subscribed to the yearly *Book of the Year* updates, and while we were in Japan, she regularly read to me from my Bible story book, a colorful and entertaining book entitled *Japanese Children's Stories* and numerous Little Golden Books. In Polo, my grandparents and my aunt encouraged my reading habit, even though they all had very limited education. I particularly remember my grandparents urging me to use the local Carnegie Library and scraping together

1. Trinity College is now part of Trinity International University, Deerfield, Illinois.

money from their meager resources for purchases at school book fairs. (*The Gray Nosed Kitten* was the first book they gave me!) As I progressed through the excellent school system in Polo, this habit of reading grew into a fascination with history. Early on I was drawn to historical biographies; as one might expect in the "Land of Lincoln," I was fascinated by Abraham Lincoln in the early elementary grades, and I vividly recall being absolutely mesmerized by the life of Alexander the Great in my sixth grade social studies class. But it was eighth grade United States History that hooked me for good. My teacher, Mr. Crear, was a good basketball coach and an excellent classroom instructor. Yes, he taught me how to play 2-1-2 and 1-3-1 zone defenses and how to make better shot selections as I came off the bench as the sixth man, but the most important gift he gave me was the opportunity to see the relevance of history. Mr. Crear made his class interesting with debates and stories that went beyond the material in the textbook, and he encouraged me to follow my interests when doing research projects. I was especially proud of my paper on presidents who had catchy nicknames and slogans ("Give'em Hell, Harry" was my favorite!) and my interpretation of American maritime history through published poetry. Although I had identified the ministry as my career goal in second grade, I graduated from eighth grade focused on becoming a history teacher.

My high school education was excellent in the sciences and most of the humanities, but unfortunately, it was sadly lacking in history. However, I persevered through personal reading and writing papers with historical slants whenever my teachers in other disciplines would allow it. Fortunately, many of them in the humanities not only tolerated this focus but encouraged it. For example, my senior English teacher encouraged me to pursue my interest in the Reconstruction era in the final research assignment for her college bound writing class, and this led to the first of what would become many interactions with the works of John Hope Franklin, one of the giants among twentieth century historians. Ironically, many of my science teachers also kept my love for history alive—not by class projects, but by encouraging me to enjoy learning. Although I did well in social studies courses from sixth grade on, I often struggled in other subjects such as math and science. But then there was this spring day in Mr. Hewes' Geometry class my sophomore year. I don't remember exactly what we were studying, but the proof on the blackboard suddenly made perfect sense to me. I vividly remember thinking, "Hey, I can do this stuff and learning about it is kind of fun." This was my "Eureka moment" in geometry, and it carried over to chemistry, English, and beyond. Although I continued to focus on history, learning in general became something I relished, and this new attitude not only led to an improved and college-worthy GPA and class rank, it sharpened my desire to teach, and specifically to teach history.

I entered Trinity College with this passion for history and the sense it would be a critical part of my life, but I had very little understanding of what it was as an analytical discipline. That changed dramatically under the tutelage of the excellent historians and teachers who made up the History Department. Professors Doug Frank, Kevin Craig, Ken Shipps, Mark Noll, and Daniel Pals each impacted my development into a student of history rather than someone who simply thought history was cool and into an analytical thinker rather than someone who simply memorized facts and used them to describe the events and personalities from the past. They gently prodded me to address the why and how questions instead of focusing solely on what happened; they taught me the research skills I needed for this endeavor; and they encouraged me to see my academic calling as an integral part of my faith commitment. I graduated from Trinity in 1977 with the goal of pursuing history in graduate school and then teaching and serving at the collegiate level.

Although my commitment to graduate work in history was rock solid, my sense of timing was blessedly wrong. During my last two years at Trinity, I assumed I would enter graduate school immediately after graduation, but I didn't begin my work at Florida State University until 1980. One reason for the change in plans was a nasty case of mononucleosis I picked up immediately after graduation and which prevented me from working that summer.

However, the most important reason was the relationship that I developed with a certain junior during my senior year. Betty Bostrom and I were initially part of a large group of mutual friends that ate dinner together and participated in activities such as traying (using "liberated" cafeteria trays for high speed runs down snowy hills during the winter), attending concerts and athletic contests, and making late night runs to local restaurants for the sustenance we needed to carry on with our next day deadline-driven academic pursuits. During the spring of my senior year, we noticed that we were usually the last ones from our group still talking at the dinner table and our relationship as friends quietly began growing into love. We were married the day after Betty graduated in May of 1978 and have been together ever since. Our relationship amazed me since due to my low self-esteem, I was very shy around women and had therefore not dated much at all in high school and only infrequently at Trinity. I always thought I was unworthy of attention from the opposite sex, and yet this beautiful, bright, and engaging woman accepted me and loved me for who I was. I was and still am amazed at her love for me, especially since once we married she too lived with the silence surrounding my mother and its ongoing effects on me and through me on her. Betty has profoundly blessed me throughout our thirty-six years together and especially during this journey to find my mother. She has seen me as I suffered from the silence, as I struggled with the resulting stunted personal development, and as I dealt, often ineffectively, with depression, anger, and pervasive sadness. In a deep sense that only she fully understands, this journey is her journey, and I am eternally grateful that she did not give up during the trying times of our marriage and that she chose, with no hesitation and total commitment, to travel with me on this quest for wholeness. One of the profound disappointments of my life is that my mother never met Betty.

May 13, 2011

Dear Mom,
 I've been thinking about this particular letter for some time. Today is our anniversary; Betty and I have been married thirty-three years. I've thought about this letter

because I want to introduce you to Betty—or at least start introducing you to her. Of all the special events you missed in my life, our wedding and marriage is the one I feel most deprived of your presence.

I really think you would have liked Betty—Dad even told me once that she reminded him of you in some ways.

We met in college at Trinity and were friends for a good bit of time before we started dating. . . . I had never really met anyone like her before. She was (and is) smart, independent, committed to good, and easy to talk to. And she didn't seem to mind when I broke out in a sweat while doing some athletic activity—a small point but I had always been self-conscious about sweating so much. In short, I felt like I could be myself around her more than anyone else I knew. We just really enjoyed being with each other, and we shared so many values and ideas about life. Like I said, I had never felt this way about anyone before, and a year later—on May 13, 1978—we were married. You would have enjoyed our simple ceremony; like yours it was simple and the cake was the highlight of the reception!

[May 15, 2011] I regret that you did not get to meet Betty or get to know us as a couple. But at least Betty now will have the opportunity to get to know you.

Love your son,

Steve

Betty and I settled into married life and worked for two years before we began our respective doctoral programs in Spanish and History at Florida State University in 1980. Once again, a number of key professors guided me in my professional development as a historian. Dr. Richard Greaves set high standards in research, teaching, and professional ethics, and he worked just as hard to encourage his graduate students to succeed, both at FSU and in their future endeavors. In addition, he first introduced me to the topic I eventually chose as the focus of my dissertation—historical responses to death and dying. Dr. David Ammerman, my major professor, taught me invaluable lessons about seeing the classroom through the eyes of students and about making the tough decisions on what *not* to include in courses since it was (and is) physically impossible to include all the important points about any era in a semester long course. I learned many other invaluable lessons about research, teaching, and the discipline of history from other professors and my peers in the graduate program.

One of the most significant of these lessons was a growing appreciation for the connection between the personal and professional sides of our lives. Watching my peers work with their major professors on the seemingly endless quest to develop an appropriate dissertation topic, and going through this struggle myself, impressed this insight into my academic consciousness. My most successful peers chose to work on topics that in one fashion or another engaged them personally; those who chose topics simply because they were available or needed to be addressed more often than not fought their dissertations for an inordinate number of years, changed their topics mid-way through their research, or did not finish at all. As I noted earlier, I eventually chose to explore historical responses to death and dying, specifically in colonial Massachusetts and South Carolina. Although this was indeed an available topic since scholars had done relatively little work in this area, I consciously gravitated toward it because I had experienced a number of deaths, and I was therefore drawn toward examining the responses of people in the past and how these responses impacted them individually and collectively.[2] I, along with others who focus on death in the past, believe that one can learn much about life in a particular era by looking at how its people faced their impending demise and the deaths of those around them. However, I was personally connected to this topic because I was beginning to sense that I had been deeply impacted by my mother's suicide. I still didn't talk openly about her death with family members except on the rare occasions I mentioned it to Betty, and I certainly didn't share my experience with friends or peers.

2. In addition to my mother's death, many of my grandparents' relatives and friends died during my time in Polo. More immediately, in the fifteen months before we entered graduate school, five members of Betty's family died, two of them tragically.

But I did start to acknowledge to myself that September 20, 1961 lived in my memory and had shaped me in significant ways. I'm quite confident that the typical graduate student does not view her doctoral research as building a platform that supports personal transformation, but as I now look back on this part of my life, I have no doubt that my dissertation did exactly that. In spite of the difficulties I faced in terms of incomplete evidence, intermittent writer's block, and simply finding the time to carry on in the midst of an intense schedule at my first full-time teaching position, I not only completed this work, I thought deeply about death and its undeniable impact on Charlestonians and Puritans—and me.

In addition to this personal/professional research connection, my time at Florida State provided another, explicitly spiritual, foundation for eventually addressing the silence surrounding my mother's death and life. The first weekend after Betty and I moved into graduate student housing, we started our hunt for a church home by attending services at the Christian Campus House ministry located adjacent to campus. "Services" is actually a misnomer since what we experienced was unlike any church service from our past. People were attired in shorts with casual shirts and flip flops mixed in with sneakers; there were no bulletins, hymnals, offering plates, pews, or ushers; praise songs replaced traditional hymns; the guitar replaced the organ; and folks addressed the pastor as Thom rather than as Rev. Miller. We were surprised, even shocked, by this informality, but the warm welcome and spiritual depth we sensed convinced us our search was over. We attended Campus House until we left FSU five years later.

The folks at Campus House gave us many gifts. We witnessed the supportive value of small groups through the meals, fellowship, and sharing at our young married couples gatherings every other week. We learned that different approaches to worship and different expressions of faith were just that—different. They did not indicate a weaker (or stronger!) relationship with Christ; rather, they evidenced the wonderfully varied ways the Lord reaches out to his followers and their wonderfully diverse responses to his grace. We saw the integration of faith and learning in action in the ways this faith community understood its relationship with both undergraduate and graduate students. Whether it was organized activities to blow off steam after a tough week or semester; specific prayers for academic choices, projects and completion of degrees; or special book studies on Christian thinkers such as G. K. Chesterton and C. S. Lewis, the folks at Campus House took academics seriously and consistently honored that facet of our lives. However, the most significant gift I received at Campus House was the quietly growing realization that God was not the stern legalist of my fundamentalist youth who was assiduously keeping track of my every fault and planning how I would pay for my sins in this life and the next. Rather, I began to get reacquainted with the God who sent that message of care through the illuminated figure on the evening of September 20, 1961, the God whose love transcends our sins and sustains us through our suffering.

Although I still had not broken the silence about my mother when we left Florida State in 1985, I was continuing to lay the foundations for doing so. As a newly minted ABD (all but dissertation), I was actively engaged in examining the deaths of people in the past and analyzing how these deaths impacted them; in doing so, I could not escape the connection to my mother's death and its impact on my life. On the spiritual front, I began to experience a deeper relationship with Christ, a relationship that was based on his grace and which equipped me to slowly chip away at the burdens of perfectionism and low self-esteem that I had carried since childhood. I still carried these burdens; I still hid them; and I still sometimes dealt with them through anger and depression in addition to silence, but I now understand that God was continuing to prepare me professionally and personally for the moment when I would finally lay my burdens down.

I had successfully completed my graduate coursework and was hard at work on my dissertation when I left Florida State in the fall of 1985 and headed to Voorhees College in Denmark, South Carolina to begin my full-time teaching career, but little did I realize that my most unique educational experience was directly ahead of me. Voorhees is a historically black college founded as

Denmark Industrial School in 1897 by a courageous Tuskegee Institute alumna named Elizabeth Evelyn Wright. She overcame threats from angry white mobs and severe financial constraints in the early years, and Voorhees developed a hard won reputation for overcoming the multiple challenges facing black educational institutions in the South as the twentieth century commenced and progressed. When I arrived, the student body numbered around 750, and a significant number of these individuals were first generation college students from rural South Carolina, a fact Miss Wright would have applauded.

I consider my three years at Voorhees to be my post-postgraduate education, and although I did not receive a formal degree, I changed in fundamental ways that will continue to impact me as a professor for the rest of my career and as a person for the rest of my life. On a personal level, I experienced minority status for the first time in my adult life as Betty and I were two of seven whites in a campus community of over 800 people. Polo was many things, but it was not racially diverse; I did not speak with an African American until my sophomore year at Trinity (which as an institution was only slightly more diverse than Polo), and although FSU was the most diverse environment I had ever experienced, I still spent most of my time there with folks who looked like me. Voorhees was therefore eye opening for me in a number of ways. For the first time, I learned about African American culture as we experienced the new sights, sounds, traditions, and flavors of the campus and local black community; for the first time, I worshipped God in a chapel program led by an African American priest; for the first time, my accent was out of place as both white and northern; and for the first time I witnessed overt discrimination based on race as it was experienced by my students and colleagues.

In addition to these new ways of viewing and experiencing what was going on around me, my perspective on history changed in fundamental and dramatic ways. As a historian, I gained a new lens for interpreting United States History, a sharpened awareness of the profound consequences of historical silences, and a deepened appreciation for the significance of place. I now realize that these changes, especially the last two, not only equipped me to be a better teacher and historian, they gave me critical insights for conceptualizing the journey described in this book.

I was the only historian at Voorhees, and each student was required to take African American History in addition to United States History and World History. Now, I had experience teaching the last two courses, but African American History was new and outside my context in terms of academic preparation. Sadly, I must admit that while doing my dissertation research on attitudes toward death, I never thought about the fact that a *majority* of the people dying in colonial South Carolina were African or African American! African American History was not on my academic radar, but this deficiency soon faded as I threw myself into frenzied preparation to teach this course for the first time. As I read as many general and focused studies as I could, as I prepared lectures on main themes and personalities, and as I dialogued with my students (who patiently encouraged this young white guy who was trying to teach them their history), I became absolutely convinced that one cannot comprehend, let alone teach, United States History without incorporating a heavy dose of African American History. This realization changed the direction of my teaching career. I have taught African American History in some form every year but one since 1985, and I now identify this area as my foremost academic interest. Needless to say, this is a dramatic change for someone who identified himself as a specialist on the Puritans before arriving at Voorhees.

One of the most exciting elements of this new field was the sense that I was part of a collective effort to redress the relative absence of African American History in traditional understandings of the American past. In a very real sense, I joined a growing group of historians and teachers who felt compelled to challenge the silence about this critical part of United States History. Part of my enthusiasm for joining this crusade stemmed from the zeal of a new convert; I vividly remember being absolutely stunned with the relevance and centrality of all that I was learning about African Americans, their systematic oppression, and their heroic resistance to that oppression. I vividly remember coming to the conclusion that one of the greatest gifts African Americans have given to the United States was their determined struggle to help their country do better by prodding all Americans to really live up to our lofty rhetoric and ideals. I vividly remember asking myself why these insights were not part of my narrative of United States History. But in addition to this zeal for new found knowledge and perspectives, there was the relevance of this history to my students. As I observed them connect or reconnect with their history, I saw them change. I saw their disbelief and anger as they dealt with the brutal treatment their ancestors endured at the hands of white oppressors. I saw them express their pride in how these same ancestors persevered and resisted slavery and white supremacy. I saw the earnest look in their eyes as they realized the ways in which oppression and resistance to oppression were still present; and I saw them diligently searching for ways to engage these issues in their lives. In short, I learned that silence about one's history leads nowhere, but engaging one's history can lead to change in the present.

My connection to African American History at Voorhees also led to a sharpened appreciation for the relationship between a sense of place and the effort to comprehend past events. Now, on one level, I already realized that place was a powerful way to connect with people from the past. As a boy, I felt the connections that came with places. I smelled the lingering scents in old barns and sheds where previous generations of Petts and Esterlys (my paternal great grandparents) cared for their animals and went about their agricultural tasks. I visited Waynesville, North Carolina where the earliest generations of Messers settled prior to the American Revolution and where my great, great Uncle Fed swam across the Pigeon River in his hundred and seventh year. I frequently and vividly experienced flashbacks to the bedroom in Sasebo where I found my mother.

I again became aware of place when I developed my dissertation in graduate school. As I formulated my topic on how individuals in early eighteenth-century Boston and Charleston faced death, place played a role in my efforts at conceptualization. As a child and an adult I had visited my aunt and uncle's house in North Marshfield, Massachusetts—a structure that dates to the 1640s; in the early stages of my dissertation research I visited Charleston in order to search for relevant documents. Experiencing both of these places connected me to the words I was reading on paper and microfilm as I did my research. I could more clearly imagine the Puritans dealing with a family death described in a diary when I remembered looking out over my aunt and uncle's marshes toward the North River, a view that was similar to what the earliest settlers would have seen as they left their dwelling to carry their loved one's body to the burying ground. After walking through the oldest sections of Charleston, I could visualize a funeral procession for one of the individuals whose obituary I had read in *The South Carolina Gazette* or whose will I had analyzed for its clues about socio-economic standing and family relationships. Wandering the graveyard at the Circular Congregational Church allowed me to listen for the echo of a funeral sermon preached by Rev. Josiah Smith on this site in 1738 and which I had read in the archives.

At Voorhees my sense of place became more than just attempting to evoke the physical settings of past events. At Voorhees, I learned that sensitivity to place could help me more fully comprehend defining characteristics of events and personalities, both present and past. I learned this lesson by participating in the Founder's Day procession to the grave of Elizabeth Evelyn Wright where members of the campus community somberly remembered her legacy as a heroic founder through a ceremony that featured the spoken word and a commemorative flame. I learned this lesson by witnessing the pride of Black fraternities and sororities—a pride that was openly and continually expressed by occupation and maintenance of their respective corners of the campus quad. I learned this lesson when I listened to my students speak about how their places in rural South Carolina shaped their lives. An older, non-traditional student made this last point in dramatic and unforgettable fashion one afternoon when he gently interrupted my lecture on the Civil Rights Movement. He proceeded to share his experiences as a participant in the Civil Rights Movement in that section of South Carolina. He had been in Orangeburg and witnessed the racial tension that precipitated the police volley that murdered three African American college students in the Orangeburg Massacre of 1968, but even more powerfully, he recounted his time on a prison road gang—his sentence for resisting oppression. As I looked around the classroom, I realized that he had the students' attention in a way that I did not, and I made the wisest decision of my fledgling teaching career; I sat down and listened to this master teacher. I later pondered what had happened that day, and I still frequently return to what quickly became (and still is) a teaching moment for me. This student was teaching his audience about the Civil Rights Movement in South Carolina (a topic that is still all too often neglected), but he taught me about teaching. He had the students' total attention that day because he powerfully linked content with person and place. He had been in Orangeburg; he had swung a pick as a prisoner on that rural county road; he had experienced the Movement in places that were familiar to all of my students, and his narrative of what happened to him powerfully transported us back to these places during the Movement.

Given this stunning example of the power of place, I began planning to teach the Civil Rights Movement through a travel study tour that would link events and personalities with the places that defined their significance to the Movement. I first took Taylor University students on this tour in 1993, and since that time, I have led twelve other tours for students and faculty colleagues. Although I have been to the sites we visit multiple times, I still feel the power of place. I feel it when we experience the eeriness of the dilapidated store in Money, Mississippi where Emmett Till's final horrific journey began in August of 1955. I feel it when we walk over the Edmund Pettus Bridge in Selma and catch our first glimpse of the spot where the police line waited for the marchers on that Bloody Sunday in March of 1965. I feel it when we stand on the porch of Dexter Avenue Baptist Church parsonage in Montgomery and see the shallow hole left by the bomb that targeted Dr. King's wife, Coretta and their first child in January of 1956. I feel it in Birmingham when we walk down the steps of the Sixteenth

Street Baptist Church and cross the street to Kelly Ingram Park just as courageous children and adults did in the spring of 1963. I feel it in Ruleville, Mississippi when I stand at Mrs. Fannie Lou Hamer's grave and reflect on her faith, courage, and determination in the face of the unbelievably brutal racism she and her fellow local people experienced in the 1960s. Those who accompany me testify that being in the exact places where key events actually happened makes the people we are studying come to life in a way that energizes their desire to learn about the Civil Rights Movement and its ongoing connection to the present.

My effort to get to know my mother through the emphasis on place that is central to the remainder of this book therefore reflects who I am. It is, at the most basic level, rooted in the fact that I found my mother's body in a specific place and grew up in another place amid silence about her death and who she was in life. But this approach also reflects who I have become as a history professor. I have come to the point in my career where I learn and teach most effectively when I successfully evoke the connections between individuals from the past and their places. I understand their actions, choices, consistencies, and inconsistencies more completely when I visualize them living in their physical contexts rather than as just abstractions on a page of a book or a document; in short, the individuals I study in this fashion become more fully human. This was my rationale for interpreting the more traditional sources about my mother's life (letters, photographs, documents, and artifacts) by journeying to sites connected with these sources; as I responded to the Lord's quiet but undeniable nudge to get to know my mother beyond her suicide, I knew I needed to meet her in the places that shaped her life.

May 29, 2011

Dear Mom,
    Tomorrow we're off for the trip west and sites that seem to be happy ones in your life . . .
    As a historian and a teacher, I've become more and more sensitive to the power of place over my career. This time, however, it's personal. I feel a deep need to connect

with you, and I feel a deep need to do so on one level through being at or near places that were significant to you or us. I know that you're not there, but I also know that you once were and that's what is important now.

I'm not ready to return to Sasebo at this point, and I doubt that I ever will be. But I do long to be where you were in happier times for you.

Love your son,

Steve

Meeting Mom . . .

3

in Jordanville, New York

My JOURNEY TO MEET my mother in her places began with a visit to her grave in late March of 2011. I knew this was where I needed to start this process, and I initially wanted to go alone. However, at (quite literally) the last moment, I realized I needed Betty to come and she needed to be part of this journey from the very beginning. She agreed. It was a quick trip; we drove to upstate New York and, thanks to some assistance from Google Maps, found the Highland Rural Cemetery just outside of Jordanville. I wrote the following letter while leaning on a large tombstone in front of my mother's grave.

March 20, 2011

Dear Mom,

We're here. Betty and I found the Jordanville Cemetery and your grave with very little trouble. It's a bright sunny—but still cool day with patches of melting snow scattered around the cemetery. You can't miss the Pett plot since the trees Grandpa Pett planted are flourishing and over 30 feet tall. They are healthy indeed, and I know he would appreciate that fact that I'm here beneath them all these years later.

I do remember parts of your funeral but not that much. I don't remember the service at all, but I do remember driving to the cemetery at the far end and stopping right in front of the plot. I rode in the jump seat of the funeral car. But I don't remember the graveside service at all or what followed. I just found a picture of us in front of Grandma and Grandpa Pett's garage dated October 5, 1961. I think we were getting ready to head back to Polo after the funeral, but I don't know.

At any rate, I really do want to find you over these next few months. I really need to—and I know you appreciate what I'm doing and my need to do it. As a historian, I often tell my students not to reduce the people they study to a dominant negative or positive trait, and I think I'm finally ready to listen to my own advice. I need to know you as more than the mother who left me and left me suffering and wondering. I know there's much more. Some good memories have already come back in these days, and being here—at your grave—is a good thing for me for the first time. Growing up Aunt Shirley or Grandpa or Uncle Joe would bring me here on summer visits, but these visits to your grave were very hard. I know they meant well, but I was hurting and embarrassed because I hadn't really talked to anyone about the way it ended. But thank God, I'm ready now. I'm sorry about all the years we missed, but perhaps I can fill them with revived memories. It's really peaceful here today—peaceful for the first time.

Love your son,

Steve

PS I think I'm getting past my anger, and that does feel like grace.

**March 20, 2011. I'm standing at my mother's grave with the notebook
I used to write my daily letters to her.**

Our journey to find Marian Pett Messer had begun. Over the
next six months, we logged over 10,000 miles as we travelled to six
cities and twenty-four sites associated with her life.

4

in Key West, Florida

SHORTLY AFTER OUR RETURN from the cemetery, I called my father, who lived in retirement in Key West, Florida. After I shared my desire to get to know my mother, he immediately agreed to help me in any way he could. Sensing that we needed to start this process by meeting face to face, I flew down to see him. Although my journey to Key West to speak with him about my mother in an open and sustained way for the first time in fifty years was not a trip to a place associated with my mother's life, it was foundational to all that followed.

As I spoke with Dad about what I planned to do, I made it clear that my primary goal was to finally get to know my mother rather than dwell on her death, and therefore my guiding principle would be to avoid blaming anyone for anything that I had experienced. I knew that I had to forgive my mother for her killing herself, my father for failing to care for me as a child, and all the adults in my life who chose to perpetuate the silence as I grew up. I knew I needed to forgive because I wanted healing not more suffering. I knew I needed to forgive because this effort would involve many family members and not just me. I knew I needed to forgive because others had suffered too. Most of all, I knew I needed to forgive because God has forgiven me, and I needed to extend this same sense of grace to others. As I explained this to Dad over the phone, I sensed his immediate relief and support.

In spite of this good start, my stomach was still in knots on the final approach to Key West and not just because of my doubt that a fully loaded 737 could actually land on the short runway that appeared out my cabin window. I worried about how this meeting was going to go. After all, Dad and I had avoided this topic for fifty years, and I was not at all sure how Barbara, his current wife, would respond. Over the years, several of my five step-mothers had not taken kindly to any mention of my mother. However, these fears quickly subsided with Dad and Barbara's warm welcome over a wonderful seafood dinner and Dad's after-dinner question, "Well, how should we go about talking about your mother?" This question started fifteen hours of sustained conversation over the next three evenings. Dad shared his specific memories of September 20, 1961 and the intense pain he still felt when he thought of that day; he shared memories, letters, and photographs that began when he first met my mother in Denver in 1951 and went through our time in Japan ten years later; he spoke about his regrets from this period and the years that followed; he answered my many questions about our life as a family in California and Japan; and most importantly, he told me how much my mother loved me. I shared my memories and my trauma from September 20, 1961, asked questions about what my mother was like and how they first met, and began talking about my experiences growing up in the silence. One of the most moving moments occurred when I told Dad about the illuminated figure for the first time. He looked stunned and relieved; stunned that I had never shared this moment and relieved that I had felt some comfort at the end of that horrific day. Although these fifteen hours did not replace what Dad acknowledged as "the decades of silence" and although we had only begun working our way through many emotional and deeply troubling topics, we clearly felt a sense of relief as the burden of my mother's death began lifting. The following letter conveys what I was thinking, feeling, and learning during these conversations.

May 7, 2011

Dear Mom,

The timeline [for September 20, 1961] was confirmed by Dad, but he also filled in a number of details I don't remember. I guess the most important to me were the details about the day as a whole and your final words before you went upstairs to the bedroom. He said he can still hear you saying . . . that I needed him. Although the context of how everything happened may indicate you had planned your death (which given the way you did it does make sense as a conclusion), you basically left us indicating your care for me. This squares with another important point Dad made—that you were deeply devoted to me and loved me deeply. I guess I've come to know that already due to many of the things I've found out in the past six weeks, but it was important to hear this from Dad, especially in the context of talking about your death.

Knowing this about you also fits with the figure I saw. (I told Dad about it for the first time and apparently it was my vision only since he didn't see it.) I now believe even more deeply that you were expressing your love and care for me, and I love you even more for doing that.

Along with this affirmation, the questions about your death and why you did it deepen, and I realize we may never find answers. But it is clear you were unhappy in Japan, but not why. It's also clear that earlier events may have contributed (your childhood, the miscarriage, your depression after having me), but perhaps only your letters will give us more of the answer, and ironically I think I'm ready to pursue that information, especially since I am coming to know you beyond your death.

So, thank you for your love. I'm so sorry you felt you had to leave us. I do miss you so very much.

Love your son,

Steve

There were many poignant moments during this visit, including Dad's emotional apology for the childhood abuse I endured from his third wife, but one of the most moving was when I realized that my last day in Key West was Mother's Day.

May 8, 2011

Dear Mom,

It's Mother's Day, and I have felt conflicted about Mother's Day since your death. On the one hand, I think it's great to honor mothers—they don't get near enough credit for what they do in raising and nurturing children. On the other hand, I don't get to honor you since you're not with me and I haven't really honored you since your death because I have blamed you for your decision to leave us. . . .

I also feel conflicted today but for a different set of reasons. Yesterday was a tough one in terms of getting to know you. I learned more about your spirit of adventure through learning more about the many cross-country trips you took with Dad or with me. These trips were no small feat during these years with no modern Interstate system and a small child. Family seemed to be important to you— foundational in a sense. You repeatedly went to Ilion and Polo. Were you focused on maintaining connections? Were they a crucial part of your self-identity?

Dad also reinforced how devoted you were to me, and I could hear it in his voice and see it in the pictures of you and me together and in the 8mm film of Christmas 1958 and my birthday party in 1959.

But the tough moments. Dad shared more than he ever has about some of your struggles with depression. Being part of this effort has caused him to remember things that he repressed—and of course he has even more to repress than I.

You wrote a letter to Aunt Vernie on the day you died. It seems pretty normal and there is not any real indication of you having serious trouble. And yet, your death does seem planned—from your timing to your words to Dad as you went upstairs to the way you did it. Were you saying goodbye to Aunt Vernie? You did seem of have a special relationship with her.

This letter is even more puzzling given what Dad shared about your earlier struggles. Your breakdown on the night you were married is alarming and telling. Why did you feel that you weren't good enough for Dad? Your three moves toward taking your own life in Long Beach are even more alarming. Why did you feel so deeply tired and articulate a desire not to keep living? . . .

And then there's the issue of children. This was an issue I wanted to raise. Did you and Dad want a larger family? Hearing that you were told you couldn't have any more children must have been a huge blow—especially since your miscarriage. Although I feel special to have been your only child, I can't imagine what you went through dealing with the news. I hope my going off to full-day school in first grade didn't contribute to your suffering.

Well, all these tough revelations. Part of me just wants to quit my effort right now, but I know I can't. I knew there would be these times and that I would learn things about you that I didn't want to learn. But I still love you more each day and want to continue. With all of your ups and downs, all of your joys and struggles, all of your nurturing and leaving, you are my mother. You brought me into this world and you nurtured me for six and a half years. You brought joy as well as great sadness into Dad's life. You are my mother, and learning about your mix of qualities helps me know you, Dad, and myself more fully.

So, the pain is still there. The mysteries are deeper. But my love for you has deepened. Happy Mother's Day, Mom!!

Love your son,

Steve

I left Key West with Dad's assurance that he would continue to help in any way possible and with Barbara's active support as well. We would continue to talk on a regular basis (sometimes four or five times a week) over the next six months, and Dad and Barbara would later participate in the remembrance ceremony at my mother's grave on the fiftieth anniversary of her death.

Dad and Barbara in front of their home in Key West, May 2011.

5

in Ilion, New York

ILION, NEW YORK WAS the first of the five other cities Betty and I visited, and it was first for a number of reasons. My mother was born there; she grew up there until she graduated from high school in 1946 and entered nursing school; she and my father visited numerous times after their marriage and my birth; and she is buried nearby. Ilion is where my mother's journey began and ended. Ilion is also where my journey to get to know my mother began and, on one level, concluded. As I noted earlier, our first road trip was to my mother's gravesite in March of 2011. At that point, I felt compelled to start this journey without visiting my mother's relatives who lived in the area. At the very beginning, it needed to be just the two of us, but shortly after my trip to Key West, Betty and I returned to visit these relatives, listen to their memories of my mother, and view photographs, documents, and artifacts associated with her life.

Marian Bertha Pett was born on August 14, 1928 as the second child of Harold and Evalena Pett. Her older sister, Shirley was born in 1925; her younger brother, Robert, was born in 1934. Her parents, my grandparents, were married in 1923.

Although Ilion was the village most closely connected with my mother's life in an official sense, she really grew up in the Gorge. As one of her classmates from Ilion High School told me, "she lived out in the country." The Gorge is a narrow seven mile glacial valley stretching south from Ilion to Cedarville that currently appears on road maps as part of New York Route 51. Its serpentine road, dense woods, babbling spring-fed creek, and steep hills towering over the valley floor make it a beautiful drive. In addition to automobile traffic, the Gorge Road is a favorite for motorcyclists and occasional bicyclists because of its twisting curves and eye-catching scenery. It is lush with the greens of spring and summer, stunning in its full fall colors, and peaceful, but treacherous, after the frequently heavy winter snows. Fishermen and rock hunters also frequent the Gorge searching for trout and exemplary mineral specimens. My grandfather bought 40 acres of land three and a half miles up the Gorge in one of its straighter and wider sections and established a residence and a farm. This homestead is where my mother began her life.

Although I spent six months researching my mother's life, I still do not know many specific details about her childhood in the Gorge. Those with the clearest memories of her during these years (her parents, her older sister, and numerous aunts and uncles) have died, and, due to the silence that enfolded my mother's life following her suicide, they passed on few memories to those who are still alive. However, my Pett relatives have been exceedingly gracious in sharing photographs that do provide more general insight into my mother's early years. Several of these show her in her first year as a healthy, perhaps even chubby, infant. Beyond these baby scenes, two themes dominate the images of my mother growing up—the outdoors and travel.

One of the earliest pictures shows my mother being propped up on the corner of a stack of lumber by an almost completely hidden person. The family barn and chicken coop are in the background, and judging from the patches of snow on the ground, it's the early spring of 1929. Although she has a serious demeanor as she faces the camera and waves with the help of her unknown assistant, my mother looks comfortable in this setting. Pictures of her enjoying the outdoors, and especially water, trace her growth during these early years. She appears on the coarse sand of a beach with a definite smile later in 1929, and as a three year old in 1931 she plays in a small lake with her sister, Shirley. In 1934, 1935 and 1937, she is clearly enjoying Steele Creek, the babbling brook which ran behind her parents' house as it cut its way through the Gorge. One of the very few stories my Grandpa Pett did pass on to me during my youth concerns this creek and the small suspension bridge that spanned it. At some point in her early years my mother fell off the bridge and broke her arm; my grandfather recounted this story several times as a way to caution me about crossing this bridge with care.[1]

My mother as a slightly pudgy infant in 1929.

My mother on the right with her sister Shirley in
the family swimming hole, 1934.

1. Although Grandpa Pett did share this story and admonition with me and although he did share his photo albums with my Polo family during our summer visits, I did not see any of these pictures of my mother as a girl until I began this project in 2011.

There are other images as well. Winter scenes of her in deep snow on toboggans and wearing snow shoes show her love of the outdoors was not restricted to temperate seasons and water in its liquid form. And then there are the farm scenes with horses, Queenie the family dog, cats, and the yearly produce from the large family garden.

My mother with her brother Robert and four legged friends.

From her infancy through her high school years, my mother clearly relished being outdoors in the Gorge. One of the happiest images of her is from the early to mid-1940s; she's standing in the Gorge on an early spring day wearing a flannel shirt with her head cocked slightly toward her right. Her arms are folded, and she's smiling with both her mouth and her eyes. She's outside and she's content.

August 17, 2011

Dear Mom,

 As we traveled up and down the Gorge on this trip, I wondered how you experienced it and how it impacted your life. It probably hasn't changed all that much since you were alive (given the spatial realities of it being a gorge)....

 Since you clearly enjoyed being outdoors, I assume that you found the Gorge to be invigorating. And although you seemed to want to strike out on your own after high school, you still seemed to love the Gorge. You brought Dad through the Gorge after your wedding, and you visited it frequently for the rest of your life. You even requested to be buried under a willow tree on the other side of the creek.

 I can imagine that you saw the Gorge as a beautiful, peaceful place as well as a state of mind . . . I just wonder what you saw as you went up and down the Gorge Road as a child and as an adult.

Love your son,

Steve

 Travel is the second defining theme of these Pett family pictures. The first of an amazing number of such images features my mother as a one year old being propped up on the front bumper of a 1929 Chevrolet by Shirley, her four year old sister. Subsequent photographs from family trips show her at Round Top on the Gettysburg battlefield in 1933; on the front porch of a tourist cabin near Oswego, New York in 1936; at Arlington Cemetery in 1937; at Gettysburg, Mt. Vernon, Arlington Cemetery, Annapolis, Ft. McHenry, the US Capitol, Cooperstown, Rochester, and Hamilton, Ontario in 1938; at the White Mountains and Mt. Washington in New Hampshire, Belfast, Maine, and Quebec, Canada in 1939; at Rochester, Hamilton College, Mt. Washington, Boston and Franconia Notch, New Hampshire in 1940; and at Bar Harbor and Ogunquit Beach, Maine and Chase Lake, New Hampshire in 1941.

My mother at Ft. McHenry in 1938.

As I viewed these photographs with my Pett family members, we realized that most of these trips occurred during the Great Depression. We concluded that my grandfather's job as a rural mail carrier and the food produced on the family farm provided a comfortable enough life to support such extensive travel during these hard times. As I viewed these images, I realized that the love of travel my mother embraced as an adult (and which I will cover in a later chapter) was grounded in these early years. Although her life was anchored in the Gorge, she went far beyond its boundaries during her formative years in the 1930s and early 1940s.

Beyond these photographs, I have only a few documents and artifacts that relate to my mother's early years, most specifically to her experiences as a student. My Aunt Marge and Uncle Bob gave me a lunch box that she used during her elementary years. It is green and of standard size with the large white initials "MP" on one side. My mother no doubt used this lunch box when she attended the West Hill School in Ilion. By the 1930s, this school, which originally had six rooms when it was constructed in 1897, had been enlarged to fourteen rooms and a gymnasium. After graduating from eighth grade at Ilion Junior High School in June of 1942, my mother entered Ilion Senior High School, and at this point it is possible to write with more specificity about her life. She was a freshman during her sister Shirley's senior year. Since my Aunt Shirley was the valedictorian of the class of 1943, my mother no doubt felt some pressure to succeed academically. According to her transcript, she finished tenth in a class of 78 with an average of 88.28. She studied the college entrance curriculum and did well in English and History (!) and exceptionally well in Latin, Biology, and Chemistry. Her yearbook entry in *The Mirror* shows a young woman with a serious expression and describes her as "A girl we like, we hear that she particularly likes to ski." This last note is the only unexpected characteristic that stands out about my mother from these records. She seemed to have had a normal high school experience in terms of curricular and extra-curricular activities, but she had joined the Ski Club and developed her passion for downhill skiing by the time she graduated. The "We Remember" section corroborates this interest when it notes that classmates would recall "Marion (sic) Pett's skiing." It is also worth noting that only one other woman in the class was remembered for her athletic ability. Although Pett family pictures do include several images of her father and brother on skis, there are none that show my mother participating in this activity. However, this notable love of skiing fits well with her early enjoyment of the outdoors, especially winters, in the Gorge and her later skiing adventures with my father in Denver.

The Gorge continued to play a significant role in my mother's life after she married my father in 1952. She insisted that they drive through it as they left on their honeymoon. Dad recalls numerous trips to Ilion prior to my birth in 1955, visits that included finding a steep and lightly-travelled road for a version of downhill skiing during one Christmas visit, meeting members of my mother's immediate and extended family, and sharing early morning conversations over coffee with his new mother-in-law in a warm kitchen immediately beneath a chilly upstairs bedroom. As I examined the pictures from my relatives, I realized my mother wanted me to know the Gorge as well. I spent my first Christmas there; I celebrated my first birthday there; and there are numerous photographs of me posing, or more likely being posed, in front of huge snow drifts with my older cousins, Anne, Jean, and Paul. My first ride on a toboggan occurred in the Gorge, and my first serious interaction with animals no doubt happened with the cows, goats, horses, and dogs on the Pett farm. We continued to visit yearly and sometimes even more frequently in the years prior to our move to Japan in 1960.

My mother and I visit the Gorge, 1959.

Although the Gorge was obviously a central place in my mother's life, she left to continue her education at Strong Memorial School of Nursing at the University of Rochester following her graduation from Ilion High in 1946. I don't know exactly what motivated her to choose this path. There are clues, but there are only that—clues. Perhaps she felt the call to nursing because of the high level of World War II patriotism present during her high school years; one woman and seventeen men are listed as veterans in the graduation program for her class, and her cousin Viola had enlisted in the WACS. If she felt called to active service, nursing was certainly one of the most direct and valued options for a young woman during this era. Perhaps my mother felt drawn to nursing because she witnessed her father's suffering as he slowly and only partially recovered from a terrible logging accident in early 1946. Perhaps cost was a factor since the family finances were stretched because of medical expenses associated with this accident; nursing school may have offered the most economical educational option since second and third year student nurses at Strong received modest stipends for night duty at the adjacent hospital. Perhaps she just loved nursing; my father and numerous classmates from Strong noted that she clearly enjoyed her training and subsequent career. Whatever her motivation, when my mother left for Rochester in 1946, she became the only one of the three Pett siblings to leave the Gorge and not return to live near the family homestead.

6

in Rochester, New York

ROCHESTER PROVED TO BE one of the most interesting locations in terms of getting to know the mom I didn't know. I grew up aware that she had been a nurse; her nursing pin from Strong Memorial School of Nursing was one of the few artifacts from her life that I possessed and actually looked at occasionally. But going to the building where she lived and trained as a student nurse, visiting an original wing of Strong Memorial Hospital where she worked during her night rotations, and interviewing twenty-two of her surviving classmates from the Class of 1949 dramatically changed my view of my mother. For the first time, I met a college student who clearly had her sights set on a career.

I'm standing in front of Helen Wood Hall. My mother lived on the third floor and attended classes here as a nursing student.

The Strong Memorial School of Nursing was founded under the leadership of Helen Wood in 1925, and by the time my mother entered her three year RN program in the fall of 1946, it had an excellent reputation in upstate New York and beyond. During World War II, Strong had been intensely involved in the Cadet Nurse Corps Program, and when my mother's class entered as part of the first peace time cohort, enrollment was starting to decline due to this program winding down and to an anticipated over-supply of nurses following the end of the war.

Student life in the nursing program at Strong was intense in many ways. The rules and regulations listed in the 1948 edition of "First Aid," the handbook for new students, as well as the memories shared by my mother's classmates, clearly indicate that Clare Dennison, who succeeded Helen Wood as Director in 1933, ran a tight ship. Between classes, studying, clinical training, and regular shifts at the adjacent Strong Memorial Hospital, one's days (and often nights) were regimented with professional preparation and duty. In addition, there were regulations and expectations relating to expected decorum for young ladies; very specific instructions on where and how one should wear the Strong nursing uniform (unique with its square-shaped hat and numerous buttons on the blouse) and formal teas on Wednesday afternoons to encourage the social graces are just two examples of this strict and focused approach. And apparently Miss Abbott, a faculty member and head assistant to Miss Dennison, had a reputation of enforcing all the rules and regulations (especially dormitory hours) with a rigor that was not always appreciated by her young charges.

And yet, as I listened to my mother's classmates talk about their experiences at Strong and as I read "First Aid," *Meliora* (the yearbook), *the Strong Pulse* (a student-edited newsletter) and other sources from this era, it was clear that these young women also knew how to have a good time. In addition to its seemingly endless rules, "First Aid" included an extensive list of the cultural, recreational, educational, and religious activities available at the University of Rochester and in the local community as well as a summary of the regularly scheduled dances and parties at the School of

Nursing. But these were only the official listings, and a number of my mother's classmates filled me in on what life was really like in Helen Wood Hall. One of my mother's friends remembers her as part of a nurses' swimming group that had the exclusive use of the University pool every Tuesday night; this group was rudely interrupted one evening by a male student who thought that it was a men's only night and came running out of the locker room nude and jumped dramatically into the pool before he realized the gender of its amused occupants. Another classmate shared their strategy for beating the dorm hours by coming through the tunnel that connected the dorm to the hospital, waiting patiently until Miss Abbott turned her head and then scampering undetected to their rooms; apparently one student with a first floor room also removed the lock on her window and allowed her colleagues in crime to enter the dorm in this fashion and thereby entirely avoid Miss Abbott as she stood sentry in the lobby and doled out penalties for late entry. There were also after hours fudge parties, and my mother was often an enthusiastic participant. One of her friends tells of leaving a plate of fudge outside their door as a bribe for the senior student who was tasked with checking for compliance with lights out and quiet hours; she was still indigent in 2011 because this conscientious, but hungry, hall monitor first enjoyed eating this offering and then reported all involved for their violation of the rules! Apparently, making fudge was a popular late evening pastime because student nurses were furnished with unlimited quantities of fresh milk in dorm refrigerators. In another example of humor, one individual remembered the following sign on their wing refrigerator: "Through these doors the biggest baloney peddlers in the world walk."

The class history in the *Meliora* and the recollections of members of the Class of 1949 also detail the lively nature of the seasonal parties held in the lobby of Helen Wood Hall. One alumna now in her 80s started singing parodies that she and her classmates made up for these functions. Turning the lyrics of the popular 1940s song *Jealousy* into a tune dealing with leprosy and performing another song with a rousing refrain focusing on the frequency with which they had to give patients enemas ("an enema here, an enema there . . .") are just two examples of their medical humor. She noted that Miss Dennison never smiled when she screened these songs prior to the parties, but she nevertheless did approve them. A skit described in the yearbook's rendition of the class history echoed this irreverent treatment of their chosen profession:

> Something new was discovered in the line of anatomy when Marie Caldwell was operated on at our Junior-Senior party. She was found to have a family tree, jack-in-the-boxes-intestines, a hair net, and various other curiosities inside her. For the secret of such an outstanding procedure, see Dr. Mellinger and her staff, anesthetist Shevchuk with her trusty mallet, and Miss Guided Scott and her shared cigarette.[1]

Apparently even Miss Dennison joined in the fun at this banquet with her poem "Diamonds are Blinding Me," which no doubt referred to the number of engagement rings popping up on members of the senior class.

This is the only candid photo I have from my mother's nursing school years. Since she is not in it and the student nurses are not yet capped, I assume she took it during the Christmas season of 1946.

1. *The Meliora, 1949, page 22.*

Several classmates mention my mother as participating in some of the extra-curricular activities such as the swimming outings, fudge parties, concerts at the Eastman School of Music, very early morning cook out breakfasts at nearby Genesee Park, bridge parties, and tennis matches (she apparently had a pretty good serve). They typically remarked that she was pretty with a small waist line (one individual assured me it was exactly 22 inches) and that although she didn't date much, she could have dated any man she wanted to. She must have expressed a love for children since the class poem entitled *Prophecy* describes her in the future as "Sweet little Pett in nursing each day/Helps little children to continue at play."[2] Her closest friends remember her as supportive if they needed help with their class work, a good partner on night duty, and someone who enjoyed discussions that went beyond nursing issues to philosophical questions and the literary works of authors such as Thomas Hardy. But even her close friends echoed the common description of her as being hard to get to know. Several classmates described her as moody and remember her sitting alone in her darkened dorm room listening to classical music (Bach and Beethoven) for hours. One noted that she suffered from terrible headaches but would not seek treatment for them. Another said that she sensed that my mother was dealing with deep and troubling issues that she would not share; although this individual was deeply saddened, she was not surprised when I informed her that she had committed suicide. In fact, she added that today she would strongly push someone like my mother to seek counseling. Perhaps it is fitting that beneath my mother's graduation portrait in the yearbook, in which she has a very serious expression, the editors chose to include the quote "Smooth runs the water where the brook is deep" from Shakespeare's *Henry VI, Part II.* When I first saw these words, I immediately connected them to her youth growing up next to the Steele Creek in the Ilion Gorge, but the more I got to know my mother through speaking with her classmates, I wondered if it related to an outwardly calm demeanor that masked deeper turmoil and secrets beneath the surface.

2. *The Meliora*, 1949, page 26.

My mother's graduation portait. I still have her pin.

As I noted in the following letter, these conversations with my mother's classmates gave me both more knowledge and more questions about who she really was.

July 26, 2011

Dear Mom,

Olga also shared some memories that were not as positive. (Author's note: I had covered Olga's positive memories in the previous letter.) She noted that you were hard to approach, kept your thoughts to yourself, hid your conflicted nature, and were moody. She also said you would spend hours at a time alone in your darkened room listening to classical music, but she later remarked that you complained of serious headaches as well.

Olga noted that you spent so much time on your own that she thought you married someone in the Navy because you would be by yourself for six months a year and could therefore stand to be in the relationship. Olga was not surprised that you ended up taking your life since you "locked" yourself in so much that people didn't know what you were dealing with.

I heard several significant points in Olga's description of you. First I gained a greater appreciation for some of the things you enjoyed doing (classical music, reading, evening walks, etc.). Second, I also heard more about traits others connected to you (being alone, not opening up, being hard to approach, etc.). I'm left with the strong sense that you were a very intelligent, pretty young woman dealing with very complex issues. I also wonder about the headaches. What caused them? Did they stay with you as you grew older? How debilitating were they?

I am continuing to see you as a very complex person whose death must have been connected to this complexity. But how?

Love your son,

Steve

When my mother graduated from Strong on June 20, 1949, she had established an average academic record; Miss Dennison noted the following summary evaluation on her transcript: "Recorded as above average in Obstetrics and in the O.R. Probably has more natural ability than she has always exerted herself to use." Marian Pett and her classmates now proudly displayed their diplomas and nursing pins, wore the distinctive Strong cap with the newly added black stripe, and donned the white stockings of an RN rather than the black stockings of a student nurse. My mom then returned to the Gorge for a family graduation party. After staying an undetermined length of time, she drove off later that summer in her newly purchased 1949 Chevy Coupe for the journey to Denver, Colorado and her first full-time nursing position at Colorado General Hospital.

7

in Denver, Colorado

MY MOTHER BEGAN HER new life in Denver by sharing a down-
town apartment in close proximity to Colorado General with two
of her classmates from Strong. Apparently, these three caused
something of a stir among their peers as most graduates initially
stayed and worked at Strong or in the greater Rochester area. I
don't know exactly why my mother moved so far away to begin her
career; one classmate thought that she may have been rebounding
from a failed relationship with a medical student. Given the lack
of any hard evidence of this relationship and what I have learned
about my mother, I prefer to think that she chose Denver because
of her love of travel and new places and her need for speed on the
ski slopes. And in 1949 what better place to ski than Denver!

The same summer my mother moved to Colorado, Norm
Messer, a young man from Polo, Illinois entered the University of
Denver as a transfer student majoring in chemistry and intending
to go to medical school. He quickly came to appreciate the contrast
between the towering and scenic Rockies and the flat agricultural
land surrounding Polo. He soon came to relish the ski areas near
Denver, and whenever he had the necessary money and time-off
from his hectic class and work schedule, he headed to the closest
slopes. But my parents did not meet as skiers. Rather, they met on
my father's first night as an orderly at Colorado General in the fall
of 1951. As my Dad tells the story, he had just started his shift on
the second floor, when this really good looking nurse said hello

to him as she walked down the hall. He immediately told himself that he needed to get to know her better, and over the course of the next few weeks, they became acquainted and started dating. Since ski season was beginning, many of their early dates were spent on the slopes of Berthoud Pass or Winter Park after sharing an early morning breakfast at a quaint little restaurant in Empire. One sign that they were getting serious was their overnight trip to Aspen later that winter. My father noted that when they met and first started dating, my mother was a better skier than he was. On one occasion when he fell and banged up his ankle while descending an especially challenging run at Berthoud Pass, she ended up completing the run while he was evacuated in a stretcher basket by the ski patrol. Their passion for skiing soon became a passion for each other, and in June of 1952, they decided to get married.

When Betty and I visited Denver on our journey, we were able to see a number of places that were special for my parents. We walked and drove the respective neighborhoods around Colorado General and the University of Denver where they lived. We viewed the old Colorado General Hospital building from a distance since it was now abandoned and surrounded by a sterile chain link fence and stern signs warning off trespassers; however we were close enough to clearly see the second floor of one of the wings, perhaps the one where my parents first met. And we visited the trailhead at Berthoud Pass, which is no longer active as a developed ski area and Winter Park, which most assuredly is.

One wing of the old Colorado General Hospital.

Berthoud Pass, 2011.

There is one more picture that vividly illustrates what I learned about my mom's time in Denver. It was taken during the late winter of 1952 when my parents took that special trip to Aspen. It shows my mother standing in front of her Chevy with her skis, and she is beaming at my father as he takes the photo. She is a woman doing what she loves with the one she loves, and that is the significance of this place and this time. Denver is the place my mom settled into her career, honed her skiing skills, and met my father.

June 2, 2011

Dear Mom,

It was good to see some of your sites in Denver. . . . The most moving site for me was the old Colorado General Hospital building (now fenced in). Although we couldn't get real close to or enter the building, it was special to be near the spot where you and Dad first met in 1951. I actually called Dad while we were looking at the building, and it was also special to talk to him while at this spot. You two must have hit it off well since you decided to get married a year later. It was good to be at a happy spot for you!

I told Dad that we can understand why the two of you really liked Denver. Even sixty years after you met, it's still a beautiful city and the locals seem to be a friendly group. I imagine between the opportunities in terms of ski-ing and nursing, this town was pretty close to ideal for you. It's good to visit these spots and gain some perspective on a happy place in your life.

Love your son,

Steve

8

in Dalhart, Texas

DALHART IS A SMALL cattle town and railroad junction located in the northwest section of the Texas panhandle. It was admittedly a curious destination on our road trip, and on one level it is a very curious addition to this book. Betty and I included it on our itinerary not because my mother had lived there or had a significant connection to anyone who did. In fact, given the evidence I have, she stayed there for only one night in her entire life, but this stopover provides a crucial lens for understanding two of her defining characteristics as a young adult—her independence and love of travel.

But before I explain the Dalhart connection more fully, some background is necessary. As I noted earlier, my parents decided to get married in June of 1952, and on October 25th of that year they did just that in the Reformed Church in Westerloo, New York. The ceremony was a small one with family members from both sides in attendance, and it occurred just one day after my father was commissioned as an Ensign in the US Navy upon graduation from Officers Candidate School in Newport, Rhode Island.

My parents cutting their wedding cake, October 25, 1952.

At this point, their plan was for Dad to serve in the Navy while completing the application process for medical school at the University of Colorado and then enter the Reserves during his medical training. By this date, my mother had already left Denver and been on the move, having taken nursing positions in Akron, Ohio and White Plains, New York so that she could be closer to Dad as he completed his naval training in the months leading up to their wedding. Following their marriage she continued to stay in motion as a new Navy wife, following Dad to Philadelphia, Pennsylvania, Charleston, South Carolina, and Long Beach, California within the next two years and continuing to work as a nurse in each of these locations.

This litany of locations brings us back to Dalhart and a postcard that found its way into the correspondence of my great aunt, Vernie Esterly. It is postmarked June 7, 1959, and my mother notes that she and I had returned safely to Long Beach after our recent visit to Polo. (She also commented that I "was a very good passenger.") She no doubt had taken Route 54 from western Illinois to Dalhart and then proceeded southwest into New Mexico the next day to pick up Route 66 for the remainder of her trip to

California. From my parents' move to Long Beach in 1954 until we left for Japan in 1960, my mother made the long trip east to Polo and Ilion at least once and often twice a year. Some of these trips were with my father, but as his sea duty assignments took him on increasingly extended tours to the western Pacific, she continued them on her own. Each of these round trips was approximately 6000 miles in length, and she did them without the modern conveniences of fully developed interstate highways, air conditioning, and GPS systems.

Although I do not have anywhere near a complete record of my mother's letters, she registers no complaints about these cross-country journeys in the ones I do have. My father commented a number of times on her willingness to travel and on the details of their trips together. Since they had a limited budget during these years and they were obviously comfortable with each other's driving skills, their most common approach when they were together was to drive straight through from Long Beach to Polo (approximately 2150 miles) and then from Polo to Ilion (approximately 850 miles) and then reverse this approach on their return trip to California. Dad described how after my birth they rigged a crib in the back of their Chevy station wagon so that one of them could keep me company and nap while the other drove through the night. On solo trips I occupied a secure place in the back seat so I could chatter with my mom, and apparently I once gave her quit a start and a hearty laugh when she realized I had been gleefully and silently flinging my cloth diapers out the window for a number of miles. As she shared this story with my grandparents, she noted that she wondered why several drivers had honked and smiled at her as they passed.

As Betty and I discussed this simple post card, we decided that it was an important clue about my mother's life, and we therefore put Dalhart on our itinerary. As we drove through the Texan panhandle, two themes dominated our discussion. First, it was obvious that my mother thought family was important enough to undertake these long and tiring journeys on a regular basis, even when she had to do so on her own. She clearly was committed to keeping in face to face contact with the Petts and the Messers, and she was dedicated to me getting to know my grandparents, aunts and uncles, and cousins. Second, it was equally obvious that my mother continued to be an independent woman, especially in the context of the early to mid-1950s. Not only did she move to Denver to pursue her nursing career, she continued working as a nurse after her marriage to my father. Not only did she develop a passion for downhill skiing, but she did so when women's involvement in this sport was much less common and accepted than it is now. And finally, not only did she learn how to drive, own her own car, and pilot it solo to Denver as a single twenty-one year old in 1949, she continued to take long cross-country treks whether my father was present or out to sea. As Betty and I entered Dalhart and saw more cattle than we had ever seen in one place, as we drove around town searching for the Dalhart Motel, and as we talked over some flavorful Texas brisket at Hodie's BBQ, our understanding of my mother grew dramatically. The Dalhart Motel had become the Texas Motel, and that simple postcard from 1959 had become a lens focused on Marian Pett Messer's travels and independent spirit. This insight about my mother not only added to my growing appreciation of how she lived her life, it would later add to my limited understanding of why she ended it.

June 14, 2011

Dear Mom,

We're on our way back to Indiana today. . . . On our way to Santa Fe, we stopped at the Petrified Forest in eastern Arizona. I don't have many memories of travelling with you, but I do have a vague one of being at the Petrified Forest and also stopping at a tourist shop on a Native American reservation. I'll have to ask Dad if these memories are in fact accurate.

I wonder what kind of traveler you were. Did you enjoy stopping and seeing a new site? Or were you totally focused on getting to your destination?

As we have driven through all the great scenery of this trip, I've wondered what you thought of the wide open vistas of the American West.

Love your son,

Steve

9

in Long Beach, California

BETWEEN 1954 AND 1960, most of my mother's cross-country road trips began and ended in Long Beach. Except for a brief interlude in 1957,[1] my father was home-ported in this southern California town, and this is where I joined them after my birth at the naval hospital in nearby Corona in 1955.

Mom playing with me in 1955.

1. My parents moved back to Denver for a brief period when my father left the Navy to prepare his application for the University of Colorado medical school. When he was not accepted, but wait listed, they decided he would rejoin the Navy, and he was reassigned to Long Beach. During this interlude in Denver, my mother worked as a nurse, and my father did odd jobs and cared for me during her shifts.

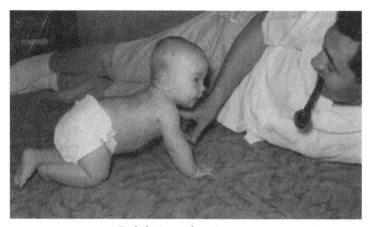

Dad playing with me in 1955.

By the time we left for Sasebo in 1960, Long Beach had become the first and only home I remembered and therefore the place associated with my earliest memories of my mother. It was therefore the only location we visited in 2011 where my actual memories from the 1950s intersected with the memories of her I was constructing from the letters, photographs, documents, and artifacts that filled in the silence about her life.

Although my parents rented two houses in Long Beach after my birth, the house they purchased in 1957 on Monogram Avenue was my first childhood home. Apparently I enjoyed my time there so much that I did not want to leave for Japan in 1960. In February of that year, my mother wrote my grandparents with some amusement that immediately after she put out the "for sale by owner" sign in our front yard, I enlisted one of my friends to help pull up the sign and replant it in our neighbor's front yard; since this neighbor was a real estate agent who had failed to convince my mother that he should list our house, he was not as amused by my protest as she was. Although I do not remember this particular caper, I do remember good times with my friends, especially Tony and Janet, twins who lived three doors down from us. We played in both of our yards, had swimming sessions in our plastic pools, attended each other's birthday parties, and shared orange juice during mid-morning breaks from our frantic activities. I must have had other friends as well since my mother humorously notes in another letter that I would wear my friends out and then go looking for new ones; on another day when my friends were at our house to play she describes being surrounded by a group of children peppering her with a million questions. In addition to playing with my friends, I remember learning to ride my first bike (equipped with training wheels) on our driveway and the sidewalk in front of our house; my mother notes in another letter that once I felt comfortable on this bike, it was a struggle to get me off it. She also mentioned we would sometimes ride together to the nearby park and shopping center. And then there were the Christmas holidays and birthday parties. As I looked over pictures and one 8 mm film documenting these events, it was plain to see that we as a family enjoyed these occasions immensely. It was also clear that as an only child, I was showered with an overabundance of presents. Dad told me that to add to the festive feeling of Christmas, he and my mother would often crank up the air conditioning to cool the house down and then start a fire in our fireplace. One Christmas Eve Dad even enlisted one of his fellow officers to play Santa and come in our back porch door to surprise me. This plan failed as I took one look at this strange fellow and took off howling for my bedroom. However, this experience was an aberration for me; my life on Monogram was a happy one.

This is what awaited me on Christmas morning, 1957.

May 16, 2011

Dear Mom,

Today we got copies of the 8 mm film from Christmas 1958 and spring of 1959. Tonight as I watched the film, I froze the frame where you came to help me at the picnic table. It was important to me to look into your eyes as you glanced toward the camera before moving out of the picture. You did love me and you did love special events and you did love having other children around! I can see all of these qualities in this film. There is a whole lot of joy on this film—it's a real gift after all the years of pain.

Love your son,

Steve

June 10, 2011

Dear Mom,

Today was another busy day in Long Beach. We visited Roycroft, N. Belmont, and Monogram (twice).

Monogram is still part of a very nice and family-oriented neighborhood. On our first trip, the owners were off to work, but we spoke with a neighbor who bought Tony and Janet's house in 1964 . . . we later returned and spoke with the owner [of our house] . . . It was moving for me because I have the 8 mm film of Christmas of 1958 and my birthday in 1959. I know there were good times there. I know where my sandbox was. I remember learning to ride my first bicycle on the front sidewalk. I remember playing in the driveway and in the front yard. I remember Tony and Janet. I remember the back yard. I have good memories of us together at Monogram and that is the most moving memory of all. I remember happiness with us on Monogram.

Love your son,

Steve

My mother's life on Monogram was, however, much more complex than the one I remembered. It is clear from her letters and existent photos that she enjoyed caring for me and she enjoyed some of the responsibilities and opportunities of home life. For example, she genuinely relished having other children around the house; she enjoyed tending the yard, her flowers (especially the huge lilies in the backyard), and the small garden that she and I maintained; she got into redecorating and especially repainting; she enjoyed sewing with the supplies from the classic wooden barrel sewing basket my Aunt Vernie gave her (and which I still have in our living room today); she participated in bridge parties and dinners with other navy couples; and she chatted frequently on the phone with relatives, her friends on the block, and fellow navy wives. She also seemed to appreciate the visits from my Polo grandparents who twice journeyed by train to see their number one grandson and his parents.

But as I researched my mom's life more intensively, it became increasingly clear she was also deeply troubled during these years. When I went to Key West, Dad told me for the first time that my mother attempted suicide twice during our years on Monogram. One time she tried to drown herself in the bathtub, and the second time she tried to gas herself in the kitchen. I have no memories of either of these attempts, and apparently in both cases, she tried to ensure my safety before attempting to end her life. She timed them when she knew Dad would be home soon, and when she attempted to gas herself, she placed towels under the door to my bedroom so that I would not be overcome by the fumes while taking my nap. When I pressed Dad about what was so awful about her life that she attempted to end it, he opened up and shared other memories for the first time. On their wedding night in 1952, my mother had become very emotional about feeling that she wasn't worthy of marrying Dad; in 1953, she had suffered a miscarriage and dealt with its immediate aftermath on her own because Dad was out to sea on an extended voyage in the Caribbean; and after my birth, she had gone through a period of post-partum depression. I then asked if they had addressed these issues before we left for Japan. His answer was that they had not since my mother usually returned to her normal self within a couple of days of each occurrence and then assured him that she was just fine. For example, Dad shared that by the time he could get back to port after getting the emergency call about her 1953 miscarriage, my mother was back to work and everything seemed normal even though she had spent several days recovering in the hospital. I suspect that the general indifference to mental illness, the social stigma attached to it, and the potential negative impact on my father's career influenced their reluctance to seek treatment. However, given what my mother's classmates from nursing school said about her tendency to keep troubling issues to herself, it was not out of character for her to assume a pose of normalcy and insist that she was ready to carry on.

As I pondered these revelations in the context of what I had already learned about my mother, I was left with a multitude of questions. Were all of these manifestations of deep personal turmoil and mental illness related to earlier trauma? Were these feelings of depression and anxiety the reason my mother spoke with my grandparents in 1959 about taking care of me should anything happen to her in Japan? Was my mother struggling with the fact that during our time on Monogram, Dad was frequently at sea on extended tours? Was she struggling with the fact that once I came along, she no longer worked as a nurse and thereby lost the stimulation and independence her career provided? Did she know about the affair that Dad confessed to me during the fall of 2011, an affair that occurred during one of his extended tours to Japan during this period and which was clearly more than a one night fling? If she did know about this unfaithfulness or even sensed it, how did this affect her?

June 9, 2011

Dear Mom,

Yesterday we also made a couple more stops as we made our way into Long Beach. . . . We also stopped at the Long Beach Public Library, and we were able to find the February 14, 1960 ad that you placed in order to sell the house on Monogram. Thanks to Betty's sharp eyes and the assistance of a reference librarian, we found the ad. It's not remarkable, but it does remind us of how independent you were. You sold this house on your own without a real estate agent! In one of your letters, you noted that you were working on this without an agent in order to save $800. In another letter you mentioned the complexities of selling a house in California. But you did it on your own while you were taking care of me and getting ready for the move to Japan. We are really impressed by your ability to do this on your own. And of course, this realization once again prompts speculation of what happened to you in Japan. Or more accurately given the mental difficulties you had in Long Beach, what were you dealing with that caused such an accomplished independent woman to consider taking her own life? Whatever it was, it must have been an awful burden, and I regret that we were not together long enough for me to help you bear it.

Love your son,

Steve

So, our visit to Monogram was both happy and sad. I immediately recognized our house and felt like I was in a familiar place even though I hadn't been there for over fifty years. The sapling where my dad parked his car in 1958 was now a full grown tree and the surrounding houses had been modernized, but it was still the street where I played with Tony and Janet and learned to ride my bike. The current owner of the house graciously showed us around, and I saw the backyard where I celebrated birthdays, played in my sand box and pool, and hung out with my friends.

But as I looked at our house more intently, I was saddened to connect this place for the first time with my mother's turmoil and suffering. In the context of this hidden side of our life together on Monogram, I'm left to wonder why my mother agreed to go to Japan when my father began a two year tour in Sasebo in late 1959. I know from one of my father's letters to his parents that initially she was not eager to accompany him. Perhaps the reason she finally consented to go was the financial challenge of maintaining a residence in California while Dad was living in Japan. Perhaps they felt that they needed to be together in order to maintain their marriage and our family stability. Perhaps she didn't want to live alone. I don't know the answer to this question, and Dad never gave me his answer. I should have asked more forcefully, but I didn't. But I do know that life in Sasebo only made my mother's struggles worse.

10

in Sasebo, Japan

SASEBO IS UNIQUE AMONG the places I discuss in this section because Betty and I did not physically go there during the spring and summer of 2011. The expense of travelling to Japan was one factor for this decision, but the deeper reason was my reluctance to experience a place so intimately linked to my mother's suicide and the pain and silence that followed. In short, I was not emotionally prepared to relive my Sasebo memories in Sasebo. However, as I learned more and more about my mother from the sources and photographs I collected, the people I spoke with, and our journeys to her places, I realized I could not avoid this place if I really wanted to meet my mom. And so, throughout this effort, I repeatedly "visited" Sasebo through correlating my memories with my father's memories and the memories my mother left me in the letters she wrote and the photographs she took between April, 1960 and September 20, 1961.

My mother's difficulties in Japan began as soon as we arrived at the military airfield in Tachikawa on April 1, 1960. In what had become an all too regular feature of Dad's life in the Navy, his sea tour had been extended, and he was unable to meet us when we arrived. What made matters worse was the fact that the person who assured Dad he would meet us and get us settled for the night failed to show. So, after an exhausting 27 hour flight from California via Hawaii with a five year old who clearly wanted to stay in Long Beach, my mother's introduction to Japan was figuring out on her own how to negotiate the two and a half hour bus trip to the Officer's Club at Yokosuka Naval Base and how to contact Dad. When Dad did meet us the next day, my mother was understandably exhausted and upset and I was very agitated. It was not a good start in Japan for the Messer family.

When we arrived at Sasebo several days later, we settled into a room at the Officer's Club as we waited three weeks for our off-base house to be completed. My mother made arrangements to enroll me in pre-school, began writing letters and post cards (starting with one of each to Aunt Vernie), and waited for our car and personal goods to arrive. By late April, we were in our house, but still waiting for the car. Our living arrangements would continue to challenge my mother for the next eleven months until we moved from this off-base house into navy housing quarters the following March. Given that we had lived in our modern American home on Monogram Avenue for the previous three years, the frustrations she expressed in her early letters from Japan are certainly understandable. We had no hot running water; we had no telephone; we had no washing machine; we had to buy ice twice a week for a *real* ice box (but I did enjoy using my little red wagon for transporting these refreshing purchases); we had no air conditioning in the summer (and I do recall a day when the thermometer registered 112 degrees); we relied on smelly and dangerously hot kerosene heaters for warmth in the fall and winter months (and I vividly remember snow falling several times); and we had to move everything we owned inside every evening to avoid theft. In addition to these challenges, my mother faced isolation from the base until our car arrived, and once she did connect with life on the base, she felt the social pressure a junior officer's wife often feels when she complained in one of her letters about having to make new dresses since "There are parties here all the time, and we are almost compelled to attend them." In another letter, she noted her frustration that she was required to help plan a welcome reception for the new admiral's wife.

Given the struggles my mother had before we moved to Japan, I was not at all shocked to learn that she began receiving treatment for depression sometime during the summer after our arrival. According to my father, this was also around the time that she found out that she could not have any more children due to an abnormality in her uterus. So, at this point my mother had the turmoil she brought to Japan, the challenges of our often rugged life style, and the realization that she could have no more children even though she and my father had clearly planned on a larger family. Based on a comment in a letter she sent to my Aunt Bernadyne on June 3rd of the following year, I also think she deeply missed her work as a nurse. After praising the then improved living conditions in our new quarters, she added "The summer pools are open now so we begin a gin and tonic partying, bridge playing summer. You are fortunate you can work, this country club living gets stifling after a while."

Although my mother's military dependent medical records were destroyed according to standard archival protocol in 1994 and I was therefore unable to view them, my father was able to establish contact with Dr. __, who treated my mother during this period.[1] He vividly remembered her case and also shared that he was at the hospital when they brought her body in on September 20th and that he later witnessed me being ushered into the room to see her one last time. Dr. __ stated that by the summer of 1961 my mother was dealing with severe depression, so severe that he had earlier recommended both more focused treatment and that she and I return to the States. He noted that my mother was not the first navy wife to experience this kind of stress in Sasebo. Life there was a challenge, and he believed the male-dominated local culture added significantly to the frustrations military wives often felt. He also affirmed a crucial point I had learned at an earlier point during my life, namely that my mother had quit taking her prescribed medication about three weeks prior to her death.

This information from my mother's letters, Dad's memories, and Dr. __'s recollections gave me a sense of context not only for

1. Although this doctor was willing to discuss my mother's case with me, I am not using his name because he was obviously deeply uncomfortable with our conversation.

the events of September 20th but for what I experienced during the last three weeks of my mother's life. Given her fragile mental state and yet another extension of Dad's deployment on the *Ajax* (he was originally scheduled to return on September 6th), two of my traumatic memories came into sharper focus. I had always remembered my mother and me staying overnight with friends and the terrible scene that erupted when she woke everyone up screaming hysterically because she had seen a man by my bed who was preparing to kidnap me. Since our friends' house was on base, the Shore Patrol quickly came to investigate and found no sign of forced entry or the presence of an intruder. In addition to my mother's piercing screams, I also remember her yelling uncontrollably at these young sailors as they tried to assure her that there was no threat to my safety. When my father and I met in May of 2011, I told him about this memory for the first time, and he had never heard of this incident. I also mentioned it to Dr. __, and he was unaware of it as well. My conclusion is that this hallucination occurred shortly before my mother's death, probably after she went off her medication. The second memory is of my mother becoming hysterical when I returned late from school one day because I had gotten on the wrong bus. I had started first grade at the end of August, and one of the changes in our routine was me riding a bus to and from my school on the base. On this day I got on the wrong bus; as a result, I arrived home much later than usual, but the kindly Japanese bus driver had calmed my anxiety and assured me that he would take care of me. I'm sure he went far off his normal route to take me home, and I got off the bus feeling thankful for the driver's care and relieved to see my mother waiting for me at the bus stop in front of our quarters. She gave me a powerful and tearful hug and then began screaming at the bus driver and blaming him for the mix-up. No matter what I or the driver said, she just kept screaming. She was in a frenzy because she thought she had lost me. These incidents leave no doubt in my mind that my mother's depression had worsened in the month prior to her suicide; given Dad's extended absence at sea and her decision to go off her medication without telling anyone, she was clearly in horrible pain. But even as she suffered and was finally overwhelmed, she still cared for me. Her emotional outbursts revealed her deep-seated fear of losing me, and her last words on this earth, the words she spoke to Dad as she went up those stairs for the last time, expressed her concern for me.

My virtual visit to Sasebo along with our actual visit to Long Beach thus gave me a much deeper understanding of the context of my mother's suicide. Although I cannot speak with clinical certainty about why my mother killed herself, and answering this question was never the primary goal of this journey, I am left with several suppositions. My mother clearly brought unresolved emotional issues into adulthood, but it is equally obvious that she had developed a strong sense of independence prior to her marriage and her subsequent change in status from single nurse to navy wife and mother. It is also clear that she carried this sense of independence into her early married life. Perhaps this is one reason for her special relationship to my Aunt Vernie, who lived, worked, cared for family members, tilled her garden, and died at the age of one hundred as an unmarried, independent, and much loved woman in Polo. And yet, even with my mother's independence, she also embraced family connections, motherhood, and the growing material prosperity of the 1950s middle class. There is no doubt that by the time she died she was deeply conflicted, and I believe one source of this tension was the gradual loss of her hard won independence in Long Beach and the rapid escalation of this loss in Sasebo. She was no longer able to pursue the career she loved after my birth due to Dad's extended sea duty and societal expectations for new mothers. Upon arriving in Japan, she faced Dad's ongoing frequent absences, the inability to maintain direct connections with family, material struggles far beyond our comfortable suburban life in Long Beach, the growing social demands routinely placed on junior officers' wives, and the strains that were growing in her relationship with my father. I am left with a strong sense that my mother was on one level struggling with what Betty Freidan shortly thereafter identified as "the problem with no name" in *The Feminine Mystique*. Although I now know that my mother loved me deeply, I also believe that motherhood and being a navy wife were not enough for her; she loved her career and her independence, and I now understand why she felt she had lost both in Sasebo and how this sense of loss must have impacted her decision to end her life.

Although the trauma from finding her and the pain from losing her will always be part of who I am, the anger I felt towards her for leaving me became tempered first with sympathy for her struggle with depression and finally evaporated into thankfulness for her love for me. I will speak more about this transformation in the concluding section of this book, but it also broadened my memories of Sasebo. As I continued to correlate my sources and memories about this place, I learned even more about who my mom was in life and who we were as mother and son.

One of my most treasured memories about our life in Sasebo was that we did spend so much time together. I remember shopping at the Navy Exchange and Commissary and my mother giving me Mounds candy bars as treats to eat on the way home; I remember walking up to an old cemetery at the bend of our road to watch Dad's ship either leave from or return to the majestic harbor below; I remember my mom caring for me as I suffered through a particularly nasty case of the flu; I remember her joy at giving me presents during her last Christmas; I remember her reading to me; I remember us planting an apple seed behind our quarters with the hope that it would one day be a strong tree; I remember her gently coaxing me into a trip to the barber shop; I remember her sailing with Dad and me; I remember her encouraging me to go ahead and dance the bunny hop with the other kids during a Christmas party at the Officer's Club; and I remember her teaching me how to identify the best options in a (to me) huge box of Whitman's chocolates located on a table at the bottom of the our stairs.

As I read the letters my mother wrote in Sasebo, I learned about other moments we shared. She describes what became my last birthday party with her as a gala affair with twenty-two of my friends in attendance; she notes that I seemed to enjoy swimming at the Officers Club and was flirting with taking a jump from the diving board; she said that one way we overcame the intense summer heat was sitting together in my small plastic pool; and she wrote about watching Japanese children going to school in their uniforms and their ritual of playfully rubbing my (to them) strange looking hair if I stood still long enough for them to catch me.

And then there were the photographs. As I examined my mother's pictures from Sasebo, I was struck by three points. First, she took a large number of photographs documenting our life on and off base so family members in the States could visualize our daily routines. Second, she had an eye for composing photographs that showed key cultural characteristics such as housing styles, commercial activities, religious sites, and common street scenes. Third, I was usually with her on her photography expeditions. The following photo is the most moving for me because I vividly remember my mother taking it as my friend and I stood mesmerized by the sight and sound of this helicopter landing at a pad on the base. I'm on the right, and I glanced back at her just before she snapped it.

The next photo illustrates her cultural eye. It shows a Japanese house in mourning.

My mother notes the following on the back, "House where someone recently died. Outside upper window hang sleeping pads. Decorations in front of tree denote death." In addition to this cultural focus, I am drawn to my mother's shadow in the foreground, especially since I have the camera she used to take this picture. She clearly enjoyed taking photographs and sharing them with others. I imagine her smiling when she saw a scene she wished to save and share on film. Perhaps she picked up this interest from her father, who took most of those family and travel photographs that helped me document her childhood and adolescent years. Perhaps she felt the need to document my childhood since the number of her photos goes up dramatically during our time in Long Beach and our first year in Sasebo. Perhaps in some way these photographs helped her deal with her inner turmoil and indicate that in the midst of her pain, she was still engaged with her life and her family.

As I examined her pictures from Japan, it suddenly dawned on me that she didn't take as many after Christmas of 1960 and there are virtually none from the last few months of her life.

As I reflect on all that I learned about our life together in Sasebo, one moment is deeply etched in my mind. We're living in our first house off-base and it's a hot, steamy summer day. I'm sitting in the shade on our porch with my mother, and she sees an old Japanese man wobbling up the street bearing a heavy load on his shoulders. She quietly gets up, goes inside, and comes out with a glass of cold water. She walks up to the man, smiles at him, and hands him the cup. He drinks the water and returns her smile as he hands her the glass. He turns and continues his struggle up the hill. She returns to the porch and says nothing as she sits next to me. Years later this memory first came back to me during a Taylor University chapel service that focused on what it means to give a cup of water in Christ's name. At that point, I began to realize that in addition to sharing a cup of water with this old man, my mother had given me a gift as well. She showed me grace and kindness in action. This revived and newly contextualized memory represents a key part of the transformation I experienced during these journeys to her places. I slowly began to realize that I needed to extend that same grace and kindness to this woman who struggled unsuccessfully with shattered expectations and depression but who loved me as her son and who I had come to know as my mom.

11

and again in Ilion, New York

As our summer travels eased into the fall, Betty and I began preparing for two more visits to Ilion. I was on an unpaid leave of absence I had requested from Taylor University in order to continue processing what I had learned and what I was experiencing. And yet, I was not the only one who needed to heal. As I spoke about my mother with family members during the preceding months, they often shared that they too had been impacted by her death and the silence that walled off her life. None of us had experienced the opportunity to share our feelings openly, and none of us had been able to honor my mother's life. We therefore planned two gatherings to welcome her back into our lives.

On August 14th, eight of us gathered at my mother's grave to honor her on what would have been her 83rd birthday. I first thought of doing this remembrance when I realized that I had no memory of celebrating her birthday even though she had clearly relished celebrating mine. I don't remember doing so while she was alive, and after her death, I didn't want to as I grew up in silent turmoil about her relationship with me. But this birthday was different due to what I had learned about her and us. After I thanked everyone for their gracious support and encouragement, we shared a box of Whitman's chocolates (one of my mother's favorite treats) to honor her. We then shared memories and hugs (lots of hugs!) and placed flowers on my mother's grave and the nearby graves of Pett and Kuba relatives. We continued the celebration by sharing a meal at a local restaurant overlooking Canadarago Lake. Many special moments made up this day, but two were particularly poignant for me. That morning during the worship service at the church my mother attended as a child, we celebrated a parishioner's special day by singing "Happy Birthday." Although I certainly wished this individual the best of birthdays, I was not singing to him that morning. I was singing to my mom. The second extra special moment occurred as we were leaving the cemetery. I was walking with Uncle Bob, my mother's younger brother. As we reached his car, he looked back toward my mother's grave and softly said "Happy Birthday, dear sister." All I could think of was Amen! As I reflect back on this day as a whole, I realize this gathering was a key moment of healing for me; with the love and encouragement of these family members, I finally felt I could openly express my love for the mother I had lost as a six year old and for the mom I had met fifty years later.

Uncle Bob and me opening the Whitman's chocolates.

August 13, 2011

Dear Mom,

    Today we left on another trip to Ilion. We're going out to join family members in commemorating your birthday.

    Doing this is very special to me because I don't remember helping you celebrate your birthday while you were alive. I'm sure I did, but I just don't remember. And after your death, I didn't do it because of the silence surrounding your life. I can't even remember exactly when I realized your birthday was August 14, but it was fairly recently. I guess this was another sign that you really weren't much of a part of my life.

    So, tomorrow we gather to remember you and your birthday. I've brought a box of Whitman's chocolates because I do remember one in Japan, and I do remember that we enjoyed it together. (Perhaps we even enjoyed it as part of your last birthday on August 14, 1961—who knows?) When we eat the candy together tomorrow, I will be doing so as part of a birthday gift to you and as part of one of the joyful moments we shared.

Love your son,

Steve

August 14, 2011

Dear Mom,

    Happy Birthday! It was special to honor you with Betty, Uncle Bob, Aunt Marge, Anne, Ron, Carol and Diana . . .

    It was especially meaningful for me to remember you on your 83rd birthday in your church and at your grave with members of your family. This was a key moment in getting beyond your death to your life and to the love that we have for you and your memory.

Happy Birthday!

Love your son,

Steve

Our celebration of my mother's life and her return to our lives continued five weeks later on September 20th, the fiftieth anniversary of her death, but this family gathering was not only about her. We first gathered at the nearby grave of my cousin Paul, who had committed suicide in 2006. Although the pain from his death was all too fresh, he too needed to be welcomed back into our memories and conversations and honored with flowers on his grave. As we carefully traversed the uneven ground between Paul's grave and my mother's, I looked at those who had come and realized how remarkable this group of sixteen was. There were members of the Pett and Messer families; there were aunts, uncles, and cousins; there were nine of us who had attended my mother's funeral (including my cousin Diana who did so in my Aunt Marge's womb); and perhaps most remarkably there was my father.

Dad and Barbara choose to attend even though just the thought of being there was deeply troubling for my father. In the days leading up to September 20th, he shared with me that the night of my mother's funeral, he sat alone in an upstairs bedroom at the Pett house, drank heavily, and vowed never to return to the cemetery. He was so angry at her and bewildered, he never wanted to see my mother's grave again, and although he visited the Petts several times over the intervening years, he had not gone to the cemetery. When Dad and Barbara finally decided to come, I told him that he and I could go up to the grave by ourselves the day before the family gathering. As we drove through the gently rolling hills between Ilion and Jordanville that morning, we talked more about my mother's death and life, and we shared our tears and pain over what happened and our relief at finally getting beyond the secrets and the silence. As we left the cemetery, Dad said that coming there together had brought him peace.

Dad and me at my mother's grave, September 19, 2011.

September 19, 2011

Dear Mom,

Lots of things happened today. First, Dad and I went up to your grave. It's the first time Dad has been back since your funeral on October 4, 1961.

Although this was a very hard thing for him to do, it turned out to be a good thing. He and I had the chance to talk about you and your death, and we were together doing it in the car and at your grave. Dad said he felt much better after the visit and that it was a good and peaceful thing to do. We cried together some, but it was good for us to visit your grave together. It was definitely part of our healing process.

Love your son,

Steve

When we met at my mother's grave after remembering Paul, we had a time for anyone who wanted to share their memories and thoughts to do so. I started by sharing what this gathering meant to me in terms of breaking the silence and getting to know my mother as my mom. Dad shared his perspective that what we were doing was long overdue and healing; Betty shared her connection with my mother through her struggle with depression and thoughts of suicide as a college sophomore; Aunt Bernadyne presented me with the Bible my mother had given her for her wedding; and my cousin Jean spoke eloquently about the journey we were all taking together. As a cold but gentle rain fell, I felt a sense of comfort that weighed against the pain and loss we still felt—a comfort generated by our collective love for my mother and our collective relief at once again speaking her name without hushing our voices.

Dad and me at my mother's grave on September 20, 2011.

As we returned to our cars and left the cemetery, a casual observer would have assumed we were part of a funeral procession leaving after a grave side committal service. But we were leaving this cemetery on this day after saying hello and not goodbye.

The silence that shrouded my mother's life began after her death in 1961; on this day fifty years later, we welcomed her back into our lives. We then reassembled at a restaurant overlooking Otsego Lake in Cooperstown and continued sharing with each other over lunch, but this was not a funeral meal. It was a healing feast.

The sixteen of us after our meal together, September 20, 2011.

September 20, 2011

Dear Mom,

 Today sixteen of us honored your life exactly fifty years after your death. After a remembrance for your nephew Paul we moved to your grave to remember you. I think it was hard for a number of us to say what we wanted and needed to say, but we spoke from our hearts about who you were and how you impacted our lives. I believe it was a good and healing thing for all of us to do.

 As this phase of my effort to get to know you ends, I'm not sure what to write. I have gotten to know you and love you so much more deeply. I've learned about your impact on my life during our time together and your ongoing impact after your death. I've learned so much about who I've become and who I would like to be. I've learned about pain, grace, love, and family. I feel like I'm a different person in positive ways from the person I was on March

95

17th. Many other people also remarked that they feel better and healed, and I think our healing and growth will only continue in the future.

So, I move on to the writing stage in which I hope to share this journey with others in hope of helping them to get beyond their secrets, anger, and blame.

I'll close by saying thank you for being my mom. I love you and it's been life-changing to welcome you back into my life.

Love your son,

Steve

Liberation

12

See the Whole

As I conclude this account of how I got to know my mom, liberation is the word that most accurately describes how I am changing. I have experienced transforming liberation as a person, as a Christian, and as a historian. As a result, I'm seeing my mom, myself, and those around me in new, more holistic and healthy ways that I trust will keep growing as I continue reflecting on this journey.

On the personal level, I may well have learned as much about myself as I learned about my mom. Most importantly, I realized that she did love me very much. I sensed this love in how she interacted with me in the photographs of us together and how she wrote about me in her letters. As I gathered and reflected on this evidence, I was stunned at the power of the numerous photos of my mother hugging me; I literally felt comforted and loved every time I saw them. Her written descriptions of how I was developing as an infant and young child moved me because I read words that revealed how proud and devoted she was as my mother. These examples of her love in turn revived a number of positive memories in my mind or gave me a broader basis for understanding the few that I already remembered. This simple realization that my mother did love me in spite of how she left me is critical to the way I now see myself. During the decades of silence I was often haunted by the question of whether my mother really loved me or not. I often wondered how she could reject me if she cared at all for me as her son, and this sentiment was a major source of the internal burdens I carried for so many years. This uncertainty clearly was foundational to the anger I expressed, my focus on perfectionism, and my lack of trust in those around me, among other characteristics. As I learned more details about my mother's depression and shattered expectations *and* as I learned about her efforts to nurture me as a child and care for me during her final weeks of horrific angst, I came to the realization that she did love me deeply in the midst of her pain and suffering. She was overwhelmed on September 20, 1961, but she was not rejecting me. This realization not only helped me understand parts of my internal life in the aftermath of her death; most importantly, it brought relief and peace in terms of knowing that I was indeed deeply loved by my mom.

On the spiritual front, I gained a number of insights during this quest to find my mom. I shared the most profound of these lessons in condensed form in a meditation entitled "See the Whole" in the May/June, 2013 edition of *The Upper Room* devotional guide. I focused on how I learned to see others in their wholeness rather than viewing them as defined by their worst moments. Of course, I was referring to the fact that prior to the journey described in this book, I had seen my mother only as she appeared hanging on the backside of that bedroom door and I had thereby reduced her life to her worst moment, her suicide. As I learned more and more about my mother, I came to understand her as a whole person who experienced thirty-three years of life *before* her death. I began to see her playing in the creek in the Gorge, taking vacations with her family, skiing down snow covered slopes, attending classes, doing night duty and making fudge with her nursing school classmates, listening to classical music (and Elvis), going on ski dates with my father, walking down the aisle as a bride, caring for patients in her ward, relishing family holiday gatherings, driving cross-country on Routes 54 and 66, caring for the trees and flowers in our yard, taking photographs, laughing with Kazuko, writing letters, riding bicycles with me, sharing chocolates with me, reading to me, celebrating with me, hugging me—and giving a cup of cold water to an old man struggling up a hill.

I also saw my mother's deepening pain and struggles in new and disturbing ways as I learned for the first time about her earlier attempts to take her life and her subsequent treatment for depression, and as I relived the two anguished outbursts I witnessed shortly before her death in this context. Although I gained a deeper understanding of my mother's mental illness, I was unable to reach a definitive conclusion about its exact source. But answering this question was never the main point of this journey. The goal was to get to know my mother, and as a result of achieving this goal, the decades old pain I feel because of her suicide and the silence that hid her life is now balanced by knowing this woman as fully human and as my mom. A few years ago as I once again silently brooded over what I witnessed when I found my mother's body, I decided to resign myself to being scarred for life by her death; I felt if I just admitted the fact I would never get over my trauma, perhaps I could at least move on with my life without flirting with depression on a regular basis. One day in August, 2011 just before we gathered in Ilion to remember my mother on her birthday, I suddenly realized that I was only half right in this judgment. The fact is I *am* scarred for life, but because I found my mom again, the festering emotional wound caused by her suicide is now just that—a scar. It will always be with me in this life; but as a scar, it now reminds me not only of the trauma I felt when I found my mother's body in 1961 but of the healing I experienced when I found my mom as a whole person in 2011.

As I experienced and processed this transformation, the Lord quietly nudged me again—this time with the realization that this is how he sees his children, as whole human beings. He doesn't freeze frame us at our worst moments and then eternally fixate on how to punish us for our sins. He instead sees us as he saw Peter, the disciple who let fear overcome faith during his short aqua-walk and who vehemently rejected Christ as he was being tortured prior to his crucifixion. The Lord sees us as followers who are more than our worst moments, and he continues welcoming us into his presence just as he welcomed a repentant Peter back following the resurrection. In short, the Lord was telling me, Steve, you need to see your mother the way I do.

And it's not just my mother. This realization about seeing the whole person is transforming the way I see myself and those around me. As I noted earlier, I have fought a prolonged battle with perfectionism and the fear that I was not good enough for God or anyone else to love. Although I had made some real progress in laying this burden down prior to 2011, getting to know and love my mom as a whole person is helping me to get to know and love myself as a whole person. I now know—really know—that not only don't I have to be perfect to be loved, I no longer even have to strive for perfection. To be clear, I'm not advocating willful sinning, laziness, or settling for mediocrity in the expectation that God's grace will magically make everything I fail at look good. I am saying that as a whole person who is created in God's image *and* fallen, as one who is fully human with all the strengths and limitations that condition entails, I can relax and get on with my life, my calling, and my service because God loves me as his child because he loves me and not due to anything I can or should do. What a relief after all these years! This insight is as old as the gospel and has been articulated by many who have preceded me (including perhaps most famously Paul and Martin Luther), so I have heard this good news many times. But I now know at the core of my soul that it applies to me.

And it's not just me. If God sees me as a whole person and not only as I am at my worst moments, as his child, I must strive to see others beyond their worst moments. I must strive to extend the same grace to them that I learned to extend to my mother; I must strive to extend the same grace to them that God has extended to me. I will no doubt spend the rest of my life incorporating this broad and challenging view of grace into my relationships with those around me; but I now understand the reality of whole-person grace as a cornerstone of my relationship with others.

And it's not just those around me in the present. As a historian, I live with people from the past, whether it's the ones I'm researching for a paper or the ones I'm interpreting to students in my classes. At Taylor University, we intentionally explore the profound complexities of integrating our faith with our academic disciplines, and early on in my career here, I came to the conclusion that one way I integrate my Christian faith with the discipline of history is the manner in which I treat the subjects I study from the past. Do I take them seriously as human beings? Do I follow the Golden Rule and treat them as I hope to be treated by those in the future who study my era? Do I judge them fairly by accounting for the context of their times?[1] I understood and taught all of these points prior to this journey to find my mother, but I now understand and teach these same insights with a deeper sense of urgency because I now see how much of my mother's life I missed because I reduced her to her worst moment. I now intentionally focus on reminding myself and my students that we must try to see folks from the past in the way God sees them. Does this mean that we don't judge because of God's grace? Absolutely not. As students of history, we must make judgments if we are to apply any meaningful insights to our present. But as Christians, we must make these human judgments after trying as best we can to understand people from the past as whole persons created in the image of God, and we must make these judgments while fully conscious of our own frailties, failures, and sins.

Although I learned many more lessons on this journey, seeing my mother, myself, and those around me both present and past as whole persons has had the most profound impact on me. I still have a multitude of questions about my mother's suicide and its impact on my life; for example, why did it take *fifty years* for me to meet her as my mom? I still have no conclusive answer to this last questions, but I have gained new insights on time and its role in my life cycle. One result of the perfectionism I struggled with during the decades of silence was an unhealthy focus on *always* being

---

1. I want to be very clear that I am *not* saying that one must be a Christian in order to comprehend this point; many fine historians who are not believers or who believe differently are models of this approach to their subjects. My point is that I take this issue of fairness much more seriously as a Christian because I found my mom and learned to appreciate her for who she was beyond her suicide.

on time and preferably early. (Betty and my students can certainly attest to this characteristic!) But as I reflected on how seemingly unconnected episodes in my life readied me for the journey to find my mom, I gained a deeper perspective on slow time. I realized that over the course of five decades I had been prepared and was preparing to meet my mom. I also realized that members of my family had been preparing as well and that we came together on this journey when we could be ready both individually and collectively. This understanding in turn led to my comforting recognition that I will always be a work in progress, and that's ok. As Christian believers, we hold to the hope that in the fullness of God's time, all will be made whole. I now believe this on a much deeper, more personal level because I've experienced an extended period of temporal preparation and waiting before experiencing the liberation that began when the time was right.

Epilogue

As I write these words in July of 2013, Betty and I have just returned from another trip to upstate New York to visit my mother's relatives. We once again went to my mom's grave where this journey began in March of 2011 and where we met as a family to remember her life in August and September of the same year. Although these last two gatherings promoted healing and broke the silence that had become so much a part of our individual and collective lives, this most recent visit was liberating in a different sense. For the first time in my life, I visited her grave and felt the simple sorrow of a son missing the mom who loved him instead of the bewilderment of a son brooding on his mother's suicide or the intense emotions of a son leading the effort to get past this suicide and the silence that followed. It was as if I were visiting my mom's grave with a settled sense of peace for the first time because she was once again fully in my life.

As I reflected on this experience with Betty, we were both struck by the fact that my mother's grave was indeed new in both sentiment *and* appearance. Prior to our visit, my Uncle Bob and my cousin Diana had trimmed the cedar trees on the Pett plot, planted flowers and cleaned the gravestones. Although these markers had been cleaned over the years, they now sparkled because of the new cleansing solution my uncle and cousin used. As a result, we all saw an artistic motif on the corner of the Pett family stone for the first time and my mother's name and her dates on this stone were bright and shiny instead of faintly visible. Uncle Bob also pointed out that the robins were singing gaily, and although birds had certainly sung during our previous visits, it was if we heard them for the very first time.

At the beginning of this book, I shared a photograph of my parents hanging laundry in Polo, and I noted that my goal for this journey was to reach out and turn my mother toward me so I could meet her as she really was in life. I end this book, but not the journey it describes, with another photograph that is now my favorite visual image of my mom. It was given to me by my cousin Anne and her husband Ron on one of our first visits to the Gorge in 2011. It was taken in Japan by a family friend several months before my mother's death. The two of us are on one end of a teeter-tooter in a playground located in our housing area. We are both smiling into the bright sun. I'm sticking out my fist as a happy six year old. My mom is hugging me as she leans in to share this moment with her son.

My mother left me on September 20, 1961, but my mom has finally returned. Thanks be to God!

Acknowledgments

As I REFLECT BACK on this effort to find my mom, I am humbled by the debts of gratitude I owe to so many. One of the many lessons I am learning is that we can do more and do it better when we work together. Given the lack of trust I have struggled with for much of my life, this simple realization is profound, and I will no doubt ponder it and act on it for the rest of my life.

My Messer and Pett families have shared in every step of this journey. On the Messer side, my wife Betty was committed from the beginning and gave grace filled support throughout; she asked insightful questions, interpreted letters and photos, joined me on the road trips, organized many of the details for our family gatherings, encouraged me to take time off (without pay!) to process what I learned, edited numerous drafts of this book, and encouraged me to continue submitting it to publishers. This story is in a very real sense her story, both in living with the silence during our first thirty-three years together and in the actual process of breaking that silence. My father, Norm Messer, provided invaluable encouragement. He, too, was gravely wounded by my mother's suicide and the silence. Although he struggled with his pain and grief once again, he unfailingly answered and raised questions; shared memories, letters, and photographs; welcomed me into his home; and joined the family gathering on the fiftieth anniversary of my mother's death. Dad experienced his own healing before his death in 2012, and his last words to me were to finish this book. Many others from the Messer family provided support, including Barbara Messer, my siblings Aimee Arreguin, Molly Messer, Laura

Messer, Nate Messer, and Saundra Fitzpatrick, my Aunt Bernadyne and Uncle Bill Snook, and my Uncle Ron and Aunt Pat Messer.

My Pett family has been incredibly gracious and encouraging in sharing their memories, photographs, documents, questions, and presence. They never hesitated even though they had their own deep pain and grief. My aunt and uncle, Bob and Marge Pett, provided photos, memories, and a green lunch box that helped me piece together my mother's early years; my cousin Diana Pett researched photos, yearbooks, academic transcripts, and locations; organized gatherings; and answered frequent questions over the phone. The Cedarville (New York) Country Store, owned and operated by Sharon Cole, became a beehive of supportive activity and conversation every time we visited. My cousins Anne and Ron Farrington, Jean and Temple Wilson, and Carol Pett all provided unfailing encouragement, answers to questions, and supportive presence. Anne and Ron also gave me the photo that awoke my understanding that my mom did love me.

My mother-in-law, Pat Bostrom, helped me interpret my mom's nursing school transcript. My list of supportive friends includes the Polo folks in North Manchester, Indiana, and the All In Small Group at Aldersgate United Methodist Church in Fort Wayne, Indiana. Thanks to Jane and Jeff Hunn, Becky and Denny Unger, Steve and Lila Hammer, Art and Phyllis Hunn, John and Joan Schell, Ginny and Bill Johnson, Carol and the late Tom Halliman, Patrick Halliman, Tammy Diehm, Noah Diehm, George and Marty Krestik, Deloras Lauterberg, Anne Marie Chamar, Linda Birkhold, Randy Metzger, and the late Cynthia Joyce. Each of these individuals came to understand what I was doing and why I needed to do it, and they listened to this story as it grew. Thom and Kathy Satterlee followed the journey from the very beginning, read the entire manuscript, and enthusiastically encouraged me to press on in telling this story; they also enabled our World Cup 2014 connection as a welcome break during the last stages of finishing a draft of this manuscript. Gary Felton, my barber, heard about this effort during many haircuts and was always encouraging. Jack and Robert Fox and Mike Doherty listened carefully and asked thoughtful questions as they supported me throughout this process. My colleagues at Taylor University listened carefully and thoughtfully as I shared this effort with them. Tom Jones, Alan Winquist, Roger Jenkinson, Tracy Hoskins, Vance Maloney, Solomon Abebe, Randy Gruendyke, Richard Smith, Carol Brown, Steve Bedi, and Faye Chechovich all encouraged me along the way. Scott Willson provided invaluable technical assistance. John and Ellen Dittmer, Barbara Steinson, and John Schlotterbeck from DePauw University listened and cheered me on when we met at professional conferences. A number of my students asked about my story and checked in on me during my leave of absence; thanks to Jeffry Neuhouser, Tristen Davis, Emma Cook, Greta Lohe, David Chiu, and Sam Carnes.

The reference staffs at the Long Beach, California Public Library, the University of Rochester Archives, and the Polo, Illinois Community Library provided cheerful and efficient assistance in finding important documents. *The Chronicle of Higher Education* and *The Upper Room* encouraged me by publishing brief accounts of my journey.

Finally, the following women from the Class of 1949 at Strong Memorial School of Nursing gave me invaluable insights about my mother and the life of student nurses during this era: Dorothy D. Aeschliman, Dorothy Dobmeier Berden, Virginia Pike Bornstein, Elizabeth Salisbury Clarke, Nancy Kummer Davies, Elsa Claudius Frost, Milred Wright Gilmour, Olga Gentile Grimwood, Janet Amendt Groover, Lorraine Cleason Healy, Jeanne Scott Hoose, Lois Newman Johnson, Brenda Eves Lingg, Carol Pfleeger McKeehan, Jane Whitman Mittlefehldt, Rosemary Brinkman Nachtwey, Jane Webb Peace, Mary Lacney Schauer, Ruth Carroll Smith, Gloria Barresi Viverto, and Lauretta Schulze Williams. Thank you for taking the time to speak with me when I called with questions about your experiences from over sixty years ago. My mother was fortunate to spend her college years with all of you.